# MONTANA
## *Highway Tales*

Curious Characters, Historic Sites
and Peculiar Attractions

## JON AXLINE

THE
History
PRESS

Published by The History Press
Charleston, SC
www.historypress.com

Copyright © 2021 by Jon Axline
All rights reserved

First published 2021

Manufactured in the United States

ISBN 9781467146579

Library of Congress Control Number: 2021934326

*For my mentor, colleague and, most importantly, friend, Paula Petrik,
who helped nurture me from history buff to historian*

# CONTENTS

CONTENTS

# ACKNOWLEDGEMENTS

*A*cknowledgements are the easiest and hardest things to write. This book would not have been possible without the assistance and support of a lot of people. Many work at the Montana Department of Transportation (MDT), and more than a few have since retired or crossed the Great Divide. At MDT, I'd like to single out Steve Platt and my longtime comrades in the Environmental Services Bureau. The MDT has been a great place to work, and much of the reason for that is the people. Thank you all. I would be negligent if I didn't thank the staff at the Montana Historical Society, especially Kirby Lambert, Rich Aarstad, Jodie Foley, Molly Kruckenberg and Jeff Malcomsen. The former director, Bruce Whittenberg, always made me feel a part of that family, and I certainly appreciate it. The State Historic Preservation Office (SHPO) has truly been my right arm over the past thirty years. While our relationship at first was a bit rocky, we have since developed a good working relationship over the years, and we make a good team. They are also a great bunch to drink beer with. Former state historic preservation officer Mark Baumler and current employees Pete Brown, Stan Wilmoth, Kate Hampton, Jessica Bush and John Boughton are aces in my book. My old friend Joan Brownell helped out with photographs, as did Mitzi Rossillon, Kristi Hager and Rob Park. Finally, I would also like to recognize one person in particular, my friend and colleague Ellen Baumler. She's been a sounding board for many of these write-ups in the past and on many of these subjects. In the process, she's helped make me a better historian and a better writer. As always, thank you to my wife, Lisa, and now adult daughters, Kate and Kira (who is a cadet historian), for keeping me on the straight and narrow and always being there.

# INTRODUCTION

*T*his book is a compilation of different subjects collected from multiple projects I've worked on over the years at the MDT. As you'll see, it's heavily weighted toward transportation topics, especially bridges, but there are some other things mixed in there as well. There is an abundance of really interesting historic sites next to the highways. I became knowledgeable about roads and bridges by necessity, but they have since become a passion that has continued unabated for over thirty years. I've included a few of the special ones here. I work in an agency directed largely by civil engineers. It is sometimes difficult to get used to that fact, but my paternal grandfather was a civil engineer who built roads, so I was used to the engineering character before I came to MDT and adjusted to it fairly easily. Over the years, I've tried to impart a sense of the past to the MDT. This agency has a history that is more than a century old and has had an inestimable impact on the state. At times, it was also a very colorful history full of interesting people and events and, in the end, produced something— roads and bridges—that is very cool and that we sometimes take for granted. I hope these stories and this book impart at least some of my enthusiasm for the place and Montana's history. It's going to be hard to retire from MDT when the time comes.

Many of the chapters in this book were originally published in the MDT's newsletter, *Newsline*. The newsletter, which is produced by the Rail, Transit and Planning Division, is published quarterly and includes information about the division's activities, pertinent federal and state legislation, guidelines on how to be safe on the highways (wear your seatbelts and look out for bicyclists, pedestrians and wildlife!) and environmental issues. Each issue also features a historical column. Since 2005, subjects have varied widely from MDT history and people to historical sites next to the roads and other miscellanea. Some are included here with supplemental information and additional illustrations. Since 2007, the MDT has also pursued an active program to recognize the historical significance of historic roads and bridges by listing some of its properties in the National Register of Historic Places, such as the Jefferson Canyon Highway. Also included are historic sites next to the road that have previously been listed in the National Register, such as the Smith Mine in Carbon County. MDT continues to recognize those places and will submit more National Register nominations in the future.

The chapters involving historic sites next to the road often invite speculation as to their origins. The stone chimney standing next to the Beaver Creek Road south of Havre and the concrete structure built into the side of the cliff between Logan and Three Forks in Gallatin County are included here. I almost hated to include them because the speculation is probably more thought-provoking than the reality. Some chapters are about things that I just think are interesting. Montana's Cold War history is a subject that is just now being touched upon by historians. The missile silos and launch facilities are, of course, the most interesting piece of the Cold War in the state, but there are many other places just as noteworthy. In this case, it's the U.S. Air Force's Aircraft Control and Warning radar stations that were once scattered across Montana to provide forewarning of an attack by the Soviet Union. Other subjects include Nick Mariana's famous flying saucer film from 1950, the first time the mysterious objects were caught on motion picture film.

Also included in this modest volume are twentieth-century ghost towns; an important but almost forgotten invention by a local boy in the 1910s; the story a nineteenth-century photograph tells about a heavily urbanized area; and the trials and tribulations of an Italian immigrant in Browns Gulch, west of Butte. All have some connection to MDT, its history or its programs. Some may ask what a chapter about postcards featuring mutant grasshoppers could possibly have to do with MDT. The answer is simple: the kid featured on the most famous of the giant grasshopper postcards went on to become a state highway commissioner during the 1960s and was important to the state's interstate highway program. Some stories I just find interesting. History is diverse, and this book represents that diversity from the perspective of the MDT's lone historian.

A federal regulation, Section 106 of the National Historic Preservation Act of 1966, is responsible for all this. The law states, simply, that when federal funds are involved, federal agencies (and designates) are required to identify what archaeological or historic properties may be impacted by their projects. The process involves identification, determining whether the sites are significant and eligible for listing in the National Register. If so, then MDT must make efforts to avoid or minimize those impacts. Unfortunately, sometimes the impact is total destruction and cannot be avoided. In those cases, a plan is developed to mitigate the loss of the site by the agency and the Montana State Historic Preservation Office. Most of the chapters in this book involve historic and archaeological sites that were identified as part of the Section 106 process. With few exceptions, MDT has avoided or minimized impacting most of the sites described in the text below.

So, in conclusion, I hope you enjoy this collection of stories about Montana's rich, colorful and interesting past and maybe take new notice of what passes by your vehicle's windshield as you drive through the Last Best Place.

# Chapter 1

# JOHN MULLAN AND
# THE POINT OF ROCKS

**M**ontana's territorial roads are still everywhere if you know where to look for them. Traces of the Montana-Utah Road, the Frenchwoman's toll road west of Helena and the Bozeman Trail are still easily detected by even the most amateur historic road enthusiast. The study of Montana's nineteenth-century roads has been steadily gaining in popularity, and many, like the Yellowstone Trail, have Internet sites for those interested in learning more about the subject. One route has been gaining in popularity with devotees from all over the United States: the Mullan Road. The first engineered road in the Pacific Northwest and northern Rocky Mountains, it connected Walla Walla, Washington, and Fort Benton on the upper Missouri River in Montana in 1860. Long segments of the road are still easily perceptible, with much of it still functioning as county roads or paralleling Interstate 90 and other highways in Washington, Idaho and Montana. The Mullan Road also has the distinction of being the first federal aid highway in Montana.

The idea of a wagon road between the head of navigation on the Missouri River and the Pacific Northwest had its genesis in the winter of 1853, when Isaac Stevens instructed Lieutenant John Mullan to seek "routes practicable for a…wagon road" across the northern Rocky Mountains. The U.S. Topographical Corps of Engineers detailed Mullan, a recent graduate of West Point, to aid Stevens in the survey for a northern transcontinental railroad route. Over the next six years, however, Mullan seems to have concentrated just as much on locating a wagon road as he did the railroad. Although a strong proponent of the railroad as the herald of modern

John Mullan conceived the idea for a wagon road between Walla Walla and Fort Benton, completing it in 1860. *MHS Photograph Archives, Helena, 954-200.*

civilization, he was just as sure of the civilizing benefits of an engineered wagon road.

Mullan's beliefs dovetailed nicely with the U.S. Army's plan for the construction of a military road between Nebraska and Oregon. Indeed, he was eventually able to sell his idea for the road to Congress by promoting the road as a military supply route. In March 1858, Captain Andrew Humphreys of the U.S. Army's Office of Exploration and Surveys ordered Mullan to construct a military road across the northern Rocky Mountains. Work on the road was delayed by an uprising of the Coeur d'Alene, Spokane and Palouse Indians, who were angry about the increasing number of gold prospectors in their country and the prospect of a military road intruding on their eastern Washington hunting grounds. It would, the tribes believed, only aggravate an already bad situation for them.

It wasn't until March 1859 that now-congressman Isaac Stevens and Mullan obtained the money from Congress to construct the 624-mile road from Walla Walla to Fort Benton. Work on the Mullan Road began on July 1, 1859, when Mullan's 230-man detachment, including 30 or 40 soldiers, left Walla Walla for the Cataldo Catholic mission near Coeur d'Alene. Because of the difficult terrain around the lake and in the Bitterroot Mountains, the expedition did not cross over the divide into Montana until early December 1859. Harsh weather conditions soon forced construction to stop for the season at Cantonment Jordan in the St. Regis Borgia Valley near present Henderson, Montana. By that time, Mullan's work crews had completed a little less than half the road.

Work resumed on the road in mid-March 1860. By late April 1860, the company was blocked by a mountain spur that extended down to the edge of the Clark Fork, making a road along the riverbank impossible. Mullan later stated that "in order to obtain the practicable elevation on account of the abrupt rocky face of the spurs, I carried the line up a ravine, until gaining 1,000 feet; I wound around the mountain sides, making the re-entering angles by gentle curves, until the entire six miles was completed."

This area was called the Big Side Cut and Point of Rocks segments in Mullan's 1863 congressional report. He detailed 150 men to work on the six-mile-long detour across the mountainside. Construction on the segments began on May 1, 1860, and continued for the next six weeks. Because of the rocks along the planned route, the work crew was forced to blast passages through some of the Precambrian stone outcrops to maintain Mullan's "gentle curves." A premature explosion in one cut partially blinded a man and stunned another. This arduous segment of the road proved the most difficult to construct for the small work detail. Although Mullan later claimed the cuts along this segment of the road were between fifteen and twenty feet wide, they, in fact, average from seven to fourteen feet in width. In 1862, Randall Hewitt reported that "not an inch more rock was removed than apparently necessary," and the cuts were so narrow that one could not walk next to a wagon passing through them. This is still largely the case along the Point of Rocks segment, which parallels today's Interstate 90 between the Cyr and Alberton interchanges.

From the Point of Rocks eastward, construction of the road progressed rapidly. By July 1, workers had crossed the Blackfoot River, and they reached the Dearborn River three weeks later. On August 1, 1860, the expedition arrived in Fort Benton, where they were met by a detachment from Captain William F. Raynold's expedition under the command of George Blake. Raynold had detailed him to travel over the newly completed road to Walla Walla. Mullan organized a second work party to backtrack over the road in advance of the troops to repair damaged bridges and improve the roadway.

Blake's 292-man military contingent left Fort Benton for Fort Walla Walla on August 5, 1860. With Mullan's 25 men working in advance, the soldiers were able to traverse the road to Walla Walla in fifty-seven days. Lieutenant August Kautz described the "Point of Rocks" segment of the Mullan Road: "Our road lay back from the river over a spur for three miles, when we came upon the river again. There were three or four difficult hills for the oxen." The Blake Expedition proved to be the only instance where the military used the road for the purpose for which it was intended: to facilitate the movement of troops between the head of navigation on the Missouri River to the Pacific Northwest.

After Mullan abandoned his pet project in 1862 to chase more profitable interests, the more treacherous section of his road west of Missoula rapidly deteriorated. In 1947, historian Alton Oviatt wrote:

> *Most of those who made the journey via the Mullan Road did so by virtue of necessity or misguided selection—not by choice. It had been constructed, primarily, as a military precaution, with inadequate appropriations, time*

*and equipment. Consequently, the line of least resistance had to be followed at all times. Work was done only where nature steadfastly refused to yield passage without human stimulation, and then, only grudgingly.*

Although the road was never used in an official military capacity again, it did become, for a short time in the 1860s, an important pack trail.

In 1862, newly appointed judge Christopher C. Hewitt led a party from Fort Hall to Spokane, Washington, over a portion of the Mullan Road. His nephew Randall Hewitt published his account of the journey, *Across the Plains and Over the Divide*, in 1906. Like many travelers do on our highways today, Hewitt commented primarily on the bad sections of the road. He wrote of the Point of Rocks segment, which the party traversed on September 10:

*Soon after our march began this morning the trail passed through a strip of pine forest and over a smooth level road until the foot of the mountains was reached; then we entered the Bitter Root range in earnest, and the road led a very winding zig-zag course, rough, rocky and in places exceedingly steep. The spurs and peaks of the mountains were thrown up in the utmost confusion, and it seemed as though the trail avoided none of them.*

The Point of Rocks proved to be an introduction to the more difficult Big Side Cut segment the party reached the following day. After an ordeal that took nearly a week, Randall concluded, echoing other travelers' sentiments, that when later asked the way across the mountains, he would answer, "Take either road and before you are half way through you'll wish you had taken the other. It was hilly and rough; it was abominable."

After 1864, the segment west of Missoula was, according to historian Michael Malone, "no more than a pack trail." Although wagons rarely traveled this rugged section of the Mullan Road, it was perfectly suitable for mules and an occasional camel train. Indeed, in the summer and fall of 1865, after gold was discovered on the Little and Big Blackfoot Rivers, Frank H. Woody reported that it "was literally lined with men and animals on their way to the new El Dorado."

Although private individuals or companies "adopted" segments of the road between Fort Benton and Missoula and maintained them as toll facilities from 1864 to 1872, the segment west of Missoula was never embraced by early Montana entrepreneurs. Its rough nature precluded its large-scale use by freight wagons and confined its use to pack animals, making it economically unattractive to potential toll road operators. The

The Point of Rocks was one of the most difficult, and still visible, sections of the Mullan Road to construct in the spring of 1860. *MDT.*

road's incompatibility to commercial transportation made it difficult for traders in Oregon to compete with the Utah companies, which had access to the territory through southwestern Montana over what must have seemed the late nineteenth-century equivalent of an interstate highway in comparison to the Mullan Road. By 1868, the western section's difficulty had sealed its fate, and it was only infrequently used by an occasional pack train. Instead, the travelers and freighters chose a much easier route. This route from the west closely follows today's I-90 to St. Regis, then north along the St. Regis cut-off highway to Montana Highway 200, thence easterly to the Jocko Valley and south to the Missoula valley. One of Montana's most widely traveled nineteenth-century sojourners, Father Pierre-Jean De Smet, reported many trips along this route but never on the Mullan Road between Missoula and St. Regis.

General William Tecumseh Sherman inspected western Montana Territory hard on the heels of the Nez Perce Indians during the summer of 1877. After touring Yellowstone National Park, Sherman endeavored to travel to Walla Walla over the Mullan Road. He felt that it was in the best interests of the United States to develop a closer relationship between the people of Montana and the Pacific Northwest, particularly Oregon. Although he initially planned to traverse the road on horseback with a pack train, Sherman decided in early September 1877 to attempt the journey with wagons. He planned to prove that the road still had potential as a major freight, migrant and stagecoach route. Sherman was fully aware that the road west of Missoula was obstructed by fallen timber and washouts, with none of the original bridges remaining. Local residents were somewhat pessimistic about his plans. Always the adventurer, he looked forward to the next leg of his journey, boasting that the poor condition of the road west of Missoula would add "zest" to an already eventful journey.

On September 5, 1877, Sherman; his aide-de-camp, Colonel O.M. Poe; and a fifty-eight-man military escort from the First Cavalry Regiment set out from Frenchtown for Walla Walla. The expedition included five wagons, six soldiers convalescing from wounds received in the Big Hole Battle, two dozen axes and a dozen picks and shovels. The first twelve miles on the road were relatively easy, but when they reached the Point of Rocks segment, the route became substantially more difficult. In a characteristic understatement, Sherman later reported that, with the exception of two heavy grades, the road was "plain, comparatively good, needing little repairs to make it practicable." Colonel Poe disagreed. He wrote that beginning at the Point of Rocks segment, the road was "very bad" as it ascended up the side of the mountain, forcing the soldiers to double-team the wagons. The descent was even worse, as they had to rope the wagons to trees adjacent to the road and lower them down the mountainside. After fifteen days of hard work, the expedition reached Walla Walla.

Despite the abysmal condition of the Mullan Road west of Missoula, Sherman and Poe were both convinced of the practicality of the road for light wagons. Eventually, in 1879, Sherman convinced the War Department to allocate $20,000 for the repair of the Mullan Road west of Missoula. Two military detachments worked east from Coeur d'Alene, and one worked west from Fort Missoula. The soldiers cleared the road sufficiently so that "lightly laden vehicles could once more negotiate this portion of the old trail." Unfortunately, the repairs to the western section failed to reinvigorate it as a major transportation route.

Both General Sherman and Colonel Poe, a civil engineer, recognized the potential value of the road despite its neglected condition. On September 30, 1877, Poe wrote:

> *Often, during that portion of the route, we remarked upon the pluck, the energy, the endurance, and the executive ability of Captain Mullan, who first made the road through the wilderness, and our admiration of the feat has not lessened by ascertaining from his report that it was done at a cost which amounted to only $230,000 for the entire distance from Walla Walla to Fort Benton. Its inception was creditable, and its execution worthy of any man's ambition. That it did not wholly fulfill the anticipations of its projector does not detract in the least from the credit due him.*

They also praised Mullan's foresight to sow grasses adjacent to the road to provide feed for pack animals utilizing the trail. Both men felt that if it had not been for the Civil War, the road would have become a major thoroughfare between Missoula and eastern Washington.

By 1890, the Point of Rocks segment was under county control and functioned as a public thoroughfare for the next seventy-three years. For a time just before the First World War, it was a component of the coast-to-coast Yellowstone Trail. The segment was bypassed in 1919 with the reconstruction of the highway on the opposite side of the Clark Fork River. Despite the relocation of the main route, the Point of Rocks segment continued to provide local access for residents living in the area for years afterward.

In 1908, a 250-foot section of the Point of Rocks segment was reconstructed to avoid conflicts with the Chicago, Milwaukee, St. Paul and Pacific (Milwaukee Road) Railroad's main line. It was constructed through western Montana, and engineers for the transcontinental railroad chose a route on the north side of the Clark Fork River just below the old Mullan Road. The proposed route, however, conflicted with the Mullan Road at the Point of Rocks segment. In order to maintain it as a county road, railroad construction crews bypassed segments of the old road. Fortunately, the 1908 realignment preserved sections of the old road. Like the Mullan Road, the realignment included blasted rock cuts and dry-laid fieldstone retaining walls but maintained the general fourteen-foot width of the older route. The Point of Rocks Road was abandoned by Mineral County in 1963 when the construction of I-90 terminated access to it.

The Point of Rocks segment of the Mullan Road is largely intact today. Except for the Milwaukee Road's 1907 detour, Mullan's original alignment and roadway standards still exist. It is still a rugged section of road that causes one to marvel why Mullan ever thought it could be an important wagon route over the Rocky Mountains. The construction of Interstate 90 in the 1960s preserved the old road—a rare case when building a highway had a positive effect on a historic resource. The Point of Rocks segment is but one part of a historically significant travel corridor along the Clark Fork River that has its origins in prehistory. From one point on the trail, one can look out over what is, essentially, a cross-section of the transportation history of Montana and the Pacific Northwest over the past 150 years. Literally at your feet lies the Mullan Road (which originated as an aboriginal trail); from there, two transcontinental railroads, the Yellowstone Trail, old U.S. Highway 10 and Interstate 90 occupy the narrow river canyon. For an old road buff, you can't get much better than that.

## Chapter 2

# A ROAD INTO THE PAST

## A SURVIVING SEGMENT
## OF THE BOZEMAN TRAIL

*T*he Bozeman Trail is fabled in Montana history, but not for particularly good reasons. John Bozeman and John Jacobs blazed the trail in 1863 as a shortcut from the Oregon Trail to the Montana gold camps. Unfortunately for them and the hundreds of migrants and soldiers who followed, it cleaved the last great bison hunting grounds of the Lakota and Northern Cheyenne Indians. What followed was a particularly ugly war that eventually saw the closure of the trail from Fort Reno in central Wyoming to the Yellowstone River in 1868 and the signing of a new Fort Laramie Treaty. The provisions of the treaty were used, for the most part, to justify the war eight years later that resulted in the Battle of the Little Bighorn. Perhaps on a more positive note, though, it may have been the only Indian war that forced concessions from the federal government.

As originally envisioned by Bozeman and Jacobs, the road would end at the new settlement of Bozeman in the eastern Gallatin Valley. With the discovery of gold on Alder Gulch in May 1863, the freighters and gold seekers extended the road to Virginia City within a short time. Today, you can follow much of the route of the Virginia City extension from the comfort of your car. Portions of it are visible at Black's Ford on the Madison River. Where Montana 84 crosses the river, you can see small islands in the Madison just downstream from the modern bridge; those are all that remains of the Scanland toll bridge. It is a rare relic of a frontier-era toll bridge. The historical marker turnout on Montana Highway 287 on Norris

The U.S. 287 turnout on Norris Hill provides an excellent vantage for viewing different routes of the Virginia City extension of the Bozeman Trail. *MDT.*

Hill provides an excellent vantage point for the different incarnations of the trail that climbed the divide from the south.

At a spot on the hillside above Virginia City to the north is, perhaps, one of the best-preserved segments of the road that can be easily accessed. Indeed, if you were to hike it, you could easily follow the trail all the way to Norris Hill and see where the notorious Joseph Alfred Slade's toll road branched off from it in 1863. The segment closest to Virginia City bears all the hallmarks of a frontier wagon road; it was not an engineered road, like the Mullan Road, by any means. The road just kind of grew from use, not from design. The road is only ten feet wide and slightly sunken from use. Rocks that were in the way were just tossed to the side and now delineate the roadway's route. From the road, a traveler gets either his first or last view of Virginia City. In 1864, George Forman, a failed prospector and day laborer in the camp, wrote from the vantage point of this segment, "On the high ridge I turned and took a last look at Virginia City and cursed the place and the day I had seen it, all my high hopes there being blasted."

The road segment is also known for its association with an infamous event in Virginia City's early history: the arrest and hanging of Joseph Alfred Slade. Slade came to Alder Gulch in 1863 from Colorado, where he'd gained a reputation nullifying the ruffian problem on his section of the Central Overland, California and Pike's Peak Express Company's route. Mark Twain, who once shared a meal with him, remarked in his classic book *Roughing It* that Slade "was so friendly and so gentle-spoken that I warmed to him in spite of his awful history. It was hardly possible to realize that this pleasant person was the pitiless scourge of the outlaws, the raw-head-and-bloody-bones the nursing mothers of the mountains terrified their children with." When Slade arrived in what would become Montana Territory shortly before his death, he was married to Virginia, a dark-haired ravenous beauty with a hot temper and reputation as an excellent equestrienne. The couple established a shortcut on the Bozeman Trail to the Gallatin Valley and charged tolls for its users. Slade may or may not have been a vigilante, but his presence in the organization would certainly have struck fear in the hearts of at least some of the road agents.

The segment of the Bozeman Trail where it enters Virginia City from the north was once a heavily traveled thoroughfare. *MDT.*

Joseph and Virginia Slade operated a toll road from their stone house a few miles north of Alder Gulch. *MHS Photograph Archives, Helena, 951-092.*

Slade's big problem, though, was whiskey. He liked it a lot and wasn't a happy drunk. His binges in Virginia City were epic and not appreciated by its more upstanding citizens or, importantly, the vigilantes. After a particularly disruptive binge in March 1864, the vigilantes arrested him, "tried" him and found him guilty of disturbing the peace. The sentence was a bit extreme— death by hanging. The vigilantes likely saw this as a chance to get rid of a public nuisance, and there were more of them than there was of him, so the odds were in their favor.

Once the vigilantes had pronounced sentence, a friend of Slade's headed for the tollhouse to alert Virginia of her husband's impending doom. She mounted her horse, a Kentucky thoroughbred named Billy Bay, and with thundering hooves raced for Virginia City to rescue her husband. She didn't get there in time. As she topped the ridge on this spot on the Bozeman Trail, she saw her husband dangling from the crossbar of the gate to the Elephant Corral behind Rank's Drugstore. Little Mary Sheehan later wrote, "When she was recognized, the men of the vigilance committee made haste to their dreadful duty for fear her presence would arouse so much sympathy among bystanders that the hanging would be stayed."

More than a few frontier roads in Montana send chills up and down this historian's spine, but none the way this segment of the Bozeman Trail does. Perhaps it is due to its association with Virginia City during its heyday in the 1860s and the fact that it's intact. Agricultural products from the Gallatin Valley and pilgrims who wanted to try their luck in the mining camp traveled this road. A few, like George Forman, failed and cursed ever having seen the place—from this spot on the road. The road provides a connection of sorts to the past. I also almost hear Virginia Slade and Billy Bay thundering down this road in a futile attempt to save her husband but finding she was too late. Roads, for some, are only a way to get where they want to go, but for others, they provide a connection to the people and places of the past.

## Chapter 3

# SCENES ALONG THE TRAIL

## A PICTURE TELLS A THOUSAND WORDS

*T*he relatively simple photograph of horse-drawn freight wagons on the next page tells a lot about the time and place where it was taken. It was shot by famed Miles City photographer L.A. Huffman. Born in Iowa in 1854, Huffman came to Montana Territory in 1879 and opened a photography studio in Miles City after first locating at Fort Keogh. For the next half century, he documented Yellowstone National Park and Native Americans and provided an invaluable record of the heyday of the Montana cattle industry.

Called "Jerkline Twelve on the Old Freight Road, 1883," this image shows freight wagons pulled by six spans of horses (including a span of white horses). A jerkline was a single rein fastened to the wagon's brake handle and then run through the driver's hand, in this case the man on horseback, to the bit of the lead horse. There appears to be another set of wagons immediately behind the lead wagons. The scene was taken along Alkali Creek on the Fort Benton–to–Coulson Road in what is now Billings Heights. Both Coulson and Fort Benton were steamboat ports, though on different rivers. A fence line is on the left side of the photograph and what appears to be a haystack that was, to use modern terminology, later photoshopped into the picture by the photographer. The rimrocks on the left are currently the site of residences, a water storage tank and the Aronson Couplet. My grandparents' house sits on top of the cliffs just to the left of the stand of trees. It is not known what was in the wagons. Freighters typically used horses and mules when the wagons carried perishable goods and needed to get to

"Jerkline twelve" on the old Fort Benton–to–Coulson Road (now Alkali Creek Road), 1883. *L.A. Huffman photograph. MHS Photograph Archives, Helena, 981-248.*

their destination quicker than the slow, plodding ox trains. It is difficult to believe today that this route was the precursor to Alkali Creek Road, one of the busiest thoroughfares in the Heights.

Alkali Creek empties into the Yellowstone River about a mile and a half east of where Huffman took the photograph. The valley was well known to Native Americans, with archaeological sites found in it dating back at least eight thousand years. Archaeological excavations conducted in advance of the reconstruction of Airport Road in the early 2000s revealed a wealth of information about the area's original inhabitants. Artifacts consisted of projectile points, knives, scrapers and bone fragments that tell much about how pre-contact people lived along this tributary of the Yellowstone. The Gallery Building on Emerald Drive, built on a cliff overlooking the creek, may have once been used as a buffalo jump. Indeed, other sandstone cliffs along the valley may also have been used for that purpose in the past.

The valley has, in fact, also been a nexus for historical events for over two hundred years. William Clark and several of his colleagues from the Corps of Discovery passed by the mouth of Alkali Creek on their way down the Yellowstone on July 24, 1806. Clark described the area, but not the creek. He commented on the "emenc [*sic*] number of Deer, Elk, and buffalo" and boasted that he killed the fattest buck he'd ever seen. Trappers and traders followed hard on the heels of the Lewis and Clark Expedition. Missouri Fur Company bourgeois Manuel Lisa established a trading post, Fort Manuel or Ramon, near the mouth of the Big Horn River about sixty miles to the east in 1807. From there, his employees—including three Lewis and Clark Expedition veterans, John Colter, Peter Wiser and George Droulliard—ranged out across the region in search of beaver prospects and customers for the trading post. In 1809, Colter undoubtedly passed by this area after his run-in with the Blackfeet at the headwaters of the Missouri River in the Gallatin Valley.

One of Montana's most notorious events happened near the site of the Huffman photograph in the Alkali Creek valley in the spring of 1823. Michael Immel and Robert Jones, both working for the Missouri Fur Company, had led a successful trapping expedition to the Three Forks and Jefferson River in 1822. They were leading a group of thirty men to Lisa's Fort (then called Fort Benton, not to be confused with Fort Benton on the Missouri) when Blackfeet Indians ambushed them. The Blackfeet killed seven men, including Immel and Jones. The Indians absconded with thirty-five of the fifty-two packs of beaver pelts the group had obtained the previous year. That amounted to about a $15,000 loss ($368,000 in 2020 dollars). Some of the packs later turned up at the Hudson's Bay Company post at Edmonton, Canada. The victims, including Immel and Jones, were left where they fell. Their bones may have later been placed in niches in the sandstone cliffs near present Black Otter Trail, later called the "Place of Skulls."

Alkali Creek was also deep within the territory of the Apsáalooke (Crow) Indians. The story goes that in either 1837 or 1838, a smallpox epidemic spread from the American Fur Trading Company steamboat *St. Peter*, which had docked at Fort Union. The terrible disease, for which the Indians had no immunity, eventually affected all Montana tribes. Two young Apsáalooke warriors returning from a war expedition found their village stricken with the contagion. One man discovered his sweetheart among the dying, and both warriors, grieving over loss of friends and family, were despondent and frustrated because nothing could alter the course of events. The young warriors dressed in their finest clothing and mounted a snow-white horse. Riding double and singing their death songs, they drove the blindfolded horse over a cliff and landed at what is now the eastern end of the Yellowstone County fairgrounds. The event was witnessed by twelve teenagers who were not afflicted with the disease. They buried the dead warriors and prudently left the camp. Great loss of life among the tribe followed in the wake of the epidemic. Today, the place is remembered by the tribe as the Place Where the White Horse Went Down.

In 1877, Gallatin Valley entrepreneurs John Alderson and Perry McAdow built a sawmill and store at the head of navigation on the Yellowstone River. They named the settlement after the Coulson Packet Line. Within a short time, other businesses moved in, and Coulson became a lively place in an area once threatened by the Sioux and Northern Cheyenne Indians. As it was perhaps the quintessential wide-open frontier town, death by violence far outweighed that by natural causes or accidents for the short time Coulson prospered. The infamous Indian fighter and cannibal-by-reputation John "Liver-Eating" Johnston served as the sheriff of Coulson for a few months. Like other frontier settlements, Coulson thrived only until something better came along. In 1882, the Northern Pacific Railway established Billings a short distance from Coulson and designated it a division point on the line. As Billings grew and prospered, it had the opposite effect on Coulson, which had all but disappeared within a few years.

One byproduct of the steamboat port was the Boot Hill Cemetery on the hill overlooking the Yellowstone Valley and the mouth of Alkali Creek. The

Coulson was a busy and violent place during its short existence. Some residents remain at the nearby Boot Hill Cemetery. *MHS Photograph Archives, Helena, 941-074.*

cemetery was utilized from the late 1870s to 1882 and is the final resting place of at least fifty-two individuals, many of whom died by violence in Coulson or in the area.

Billings Heights originated as an irrigated agricultural area centered on what became known as the Billings Bench. Like its parent city, Billings, the Heights experienced a boom in the years following World War II. Main Street was originally a part of the Tongue River Road between the Gallatin Valley and Miles City. In the years preceding the First World War, it was part of the famed Yellowstone Trail and was known as U.S. Highway 10 by the 1930s. Initially, businesses along its length were dominated by motels, drive-in restaurants, service stations and agricultural implement dealers. After the war, the empty spaces infilled with grocery stores, pharmacies and other enterprises that catered to the growing number of people establishing homes in the Heights. The growth has been steady over the years until, by the 1980s, Main Street was the busiest thoroughfare in the state.

With its origin as an aboriginal trail and, later, freight and stage road, Alkali Creek Road was absorbed into Billings Heights in the late twentieth century. Today, the road provides access to residential areas and schools. The road once traveled by jerkline freight wagons drawn by impressive spans of horses is long gone. But Alkali Creek Road is truly a highway through thousands of years of history.

## Chapter 4

# GATEWAY TO NORTHWEST MONTANA

## THE OLD STEEL BRIDGE

*T*oday, people take bridges for granted. While once relatively rare on the landscape, bridges now are ubiquitous and easy to construct with materials that are easy to obtain. A bridge can be built in a few days and last for an indeterminate amount of time. But that wasn't always the case. Bridges were a big deal, a much sought-after benefit that could make or break a community or area. In many ways, they were like the railroads. Build a bridge in the wrong place and a community could wither away to the benefit of some other town. Steel bridges were expensive to build, and the materials had to be shipped in from the Midwest. Communities along the railroads were the first to benefit from steel bridge technology beginning in the late nineteenth century. From those points, bridges were built in more remote areas until sophisticated systems of roads and bridges wove Montana and its neighboring states together into interstate highway systems that connected the Treasure State with national markets. In the case of the Old Steel Bridge in northwestern Montana, a bridge quite literally changed the face of the region and allowed Kalispell to grow and flourish, while the less fortunate Demersville, once the apple of the region's eye, faded away and disappeared.

The Old Steel Bridge was the first of several steel truss bridges to be constructed in and around Kalispell from 1894 to 1911. Local agitation for the construction of a steel bridge at a central point in the upper valley began in May 1893. Led by the Kalispell Townsite Company and newspaper publisher H.J. Mock, boosters advocated a special election to fund a $30,000 bond for the construction of a steel bridge. By early 1893, the townsite company had established a ferry at the site of the proposed bridge. High water, however, frequently rendered the ferry inoperable and forced "eastsiders" to cross the river by whatever means they could find. The townsite company was also opposed by residents living near the mouth of Bad Rock Canyon who believed the bridge would only benefit Kalispell and not them. In June 1893, Kalispell businessmen and entrepreneurs held a meeting at the city hall to discuss a proposed bond election. The attendees determined that a bridge "would benefit every person on the fertile east side as well as people from the west side. Kalispell is the nearest trading point for the majority of eastsiders, and a bridge across the river would be a great benefit to every rancher in this county." To prove its point, the townsite company and county commissioners hired the San Francisco Bridge Company to provide an estimate of the cost of a bridge across the Flathead River. It estimated that a steel bridge at the site of the Kalispell Ferry would cost $21,000, well below the $50,000 estimate claimed by the Bad Rock Canyon malcontents.

The townsite company was the driving force behind the construction of the bridge. Formed in 1890, the company's board of directors was composed of local entrepreneur Charles E. Conrad and Great Northern Railway executives such as J.B. Connor, W.B. Clough and J.A. Coram. By January 1894, the company had spent over $9,000 constructing roads leading to the proposed bridge site. The company solicited signatures on a petition to build a Flathead River bridge and donated funds toward its construction. On February 14, 1894, the county authorized the county clerk to advertise for the construction of either an all-steel or combination steel-and-wood bridge across the river. County surveyor C.P. Smith specified the length and width of the bridge, but it was up to bidders to develop the details. It is likely the commissioners and townsite company officials specifically wanted a Minnesota-based bridge contractor to construct the bridge, as a duplicate set of the plans and specifications were available from the Great Northern Railway's office in St. Paul.

Although the deadline for proposals was February 20, the county commissioners did not meet to consider them until four days later. Fifteen companies submitted bids to construct the bridge, including O.E. Peppard of Missoula and Lewis Gillette, president of the Gillette-Herzog Manufacturing Company, both of whom visited the bridge site the previous week. Bids for the bridge ranged from a high of $18,504 submitted by the Milwaukee Bridge and Iron Works to a low of $9,600 proposed by Hugh L. Cooper. At an evening meeting, the commissioners rejected all bids except those

In the 1890s, Flathead County embarked on a program to replace river ferries with steel bridges, including the Old Steel Bridge. *Kristi Hager Photograph, MDT.*

submitted by Peppard, the Gillette-Herzog company and Porter Brothers of Spokane, Washington. Three weeks later, the commissioners awarded the contract to Gillette-Herzog for $17,497. The Kalispell Townsite Company contributed $7,500 to the bridge, while the county picked up the remaining $9,997. The *Kalispell Graphic* later crowed, "The bridge will not only be a strong crossing but an imposing structure which will withstand the strong currant [*sic*] of the Flathead for years to come."

High water prevented Gillette-Herzog from beginning construction of the bridge piers until mid-July 1894. Company foreman McLean supervised a thirty-five-man work crew largely made up of workers hired in Flathead County. Three of the men were divers, who excavated the foundations of the bridge. The work was slow, "as the [piers] have to be sunk seven feet below the bed of the river and all the excavating has to be done by divers who can work only a two-and-a-half hour shift at a time." Because of the current and depth of the river, the cylindrical steel piers were not all erected until late September 1894. The laborious work of constructing the piers generated complaints from observers that work was too slow and the bridge would not be completed by the deadline. The first of the steel through truss spans, however, was built onshore and raised into place by a crane in early September. Once the piers were completed, work on the remaining two spans was rapid. The Old Steel Bridge was completed and opened, with no fanfare, on October 19, 1894.

The completion of the bridge spelled the doom of the numerous river ferries that surrounded Kalispell. The Egan Ferry just downstream of it ceased operations in 1894, while the nearby Penny Ferry closed down by 1900. Only the Holt Ferry remained in operation into the twentieth century, finally replaced by a timber structure in 1942.

The construction of steel bridges also changed the pattern of roads that provided access to Kalispell. With the completion of the Old Steel Bridge, the old stage road between the Holt and Egan Ferries changed to accommodate the better route across the bridge, contributing to the Egan community's eventual demise. The bridge and relocated Holt Stage Road became the primary access into Kalispell from Bigfork and, by 1914, Columbia Falls and Creston as well. The route across the bridge was, until 1936, the only access between Kalispell and Glacier National Park. According to historian Kathy McKay, "For decades the main east–west route through Kalispell followed Whalebone Drive to Meridian Road [the town of Ashley's old main street], passed through town along Second Street and exited the east along Conrad Drive, across the Steel Bridge." Both the Theodore Roosevelt International Highway (now U.S. Highway 2) and the National Park-to-Park Highway accessed Kalispell from the east over the Flathead River Bridge after 1921. The bridge was a frequent subject of postcards taken in the Kalispell area.

The first real boom in automobile tourism occurred in northwest Montana in the 1920s, largely sparked by the completion of the interstate Roosevelt and Park-to-Park Highways. In 1925, Byron J. McIntire donated land he had homesteaded adjacent to the Flathead River west of the bridge in 1897 to the Kalispell Kiwanis Club to prevent it from falling into the hands of loggers and other developers. Both McIntire and the Kiwanis saw the bridge and the land adjacent to it as one of the local "splendors with which Nature [sic] has so generously endowed us" and sought to preserve it for future generations. To that end, the Kiwanis Club, with donated material and labor from Kalispell businessmen, removed all advertisement signs from trees along the road, filled in a gravel pit north of the west approach to the bridge and planted yellow roses next to the road. Club members also cleaned out the dead timber and developed picnic sites for public use next to the river. Finally, the club erected a cedar log arch across the highway with signs reading "Kiwanis Lane" and "Kalispell Wishes You Good Luck" attached to it. The Kiwanis Club opened the park in the late spring of 1926: "The public is extended a cordial invitation to make use of the beaches and picnic grounds, and the Kiwanis Club is privileged by the same token to have rendered a fitting tribute to the beautiful valley in which we live."

As late as the 1940s, Kootenai Indians camped around the bridge, adding to the local flavor for tourists coming from and going to Glacier Park. The Kiwanis Lane park eventually grew to include land on both sides of the Flathead River in the immediate vicinity of the bridge. By 1973, however, the club could no longer adequately take care of the property, and it was deeded over to the Montana Department of Fish, Wildlife and Parks for use as a public fishing access site.

By 1929, the Kalispell Chamber of Commerce claimed that nearly all the roads in and around the city had been paved or improved in some way, adding that the "whole district is covered by a splendid network of highways and laterals that lead to neighboring towns through immense forests, across rolling valley lands and into favorite haunts, where fish and game abound, or where the picnic lunch can be spread upon grassy flats in shaded glades."

With the realignment of U.S. Highway 2 in 1936 and the construction of a new steel deck truss bridge across the Flathead River about one mile upstream, the old steel bridge was relegated to the status of being located on a county-owned "lateral." Its new status, however, made it even more suitable as a component of Kalispell's recreation and leisure industries. Unfortunately, the bridge had seen its heyday by the late twentieth century. It was way past its prime and beyond the forty or fifty years it was intended to stand. It was narrow, the wood deck had deteriorated and only one car at a time was supposed to use it—a rule that wasn't often followed. It vibrated when vehicles used it, causing a certain amount of concern for its users. The county periodically closed the bridge as a safety precaution. The problem was intensified by the presence of a popular park on one side and a fishing access site on the other. By the 1990s, the bridge was worn out, and it was demolished. Its successor, built on the same site, now serves hundreds of picnickers, sunbathers, boaters and fishermen each year—just as the Old Steel Bridge faithfully did for over a century.

Chapter 5

# THE GHOST OF CHANCE

*S*eeking out historic and archaeological resources is a big responsibility for the Montana Department of Transportation's cultural resource crew. The "work" sometimes involves travel to remote corners of the state in search of places that tell Montana's story—both colorful and mundane. Sometimes the vestiges of towns that were once prosperous communities are located next to the state's primary and secondary highways. Some of these places are beyond ghost towns; no observable remnant remains to remind people in the twenty-first century that they were once vibrant communities populated by families who came to the state to look for new opportunities. Mondak in Roosevelt County, Verona in Chouteau County and Beebe in Custer County are good examples of places that have disappeared from Montana's landscape and are fading memories.

One such place is Chance. Named for the first non-Indian settler in the area, the name also implies the risks its residents once took settling there. The community thrived for only a short time in the 1890s and early 1900s. The former townsite is along the Clark's Fork of the Yellowstone about nine miles south of Belfry. It is not on Montana Highway 72 but on a dirt road about a mile north of the Wyoming border. A circa 1965 ranch-style house occupies the former townsite; a few other buildings are scattered around the area that once may have been part of the community. Chance today is surrounded by irrigated sugar beet fields. It was once dominated by a steel truss bridge that crossed the Clark's Fork of the Yellowstone.

The Clark's Fork Valley was once part of the Crow Indian Reservation. In October 1892, the tribe ceded land from the reservation's current western boundary west to the Boulder River and south of the Yellowstone River. Non-Indians swarmed into the ceded area shortly thereafter and established homesteads on the choice lands in the river bottoms. Even before the Apsáalooke (Crow) ceded the land, however, Nathan Chance had settled on a choice spot on the Clark's Fork of the Yellowstone river bottom. Chance was a thirty-five-year-old native of Iowa who came to Montana in the late 1880s from Kansas. It wasn't until 1899 that he filed on a 143-acre homestead and built a rudimentary wagon bridge across the Clark's Fork of the Yellowstone at an ancient river ford. Chance's family included his wife, Ellen, and their children, Lillie and Quincy. In 1898, the federal government authorized Chance to open a post office in the general store that sat on his property. Lillie was the settlement's first postmaster. The settlement was located on the trail between Meeteetsee, Wyoming, and Red Lodge; a stagecoach passed through Chance three times a week.

In January 1901, Chance sold twenty acres of his land to Ludlow B. Reno, the Carbon County attorney. The sale, which was just north of the first Chance Bridge, included the post office. Reno planned to survey a portion of the tract for a townsite and build a new general store. At the time Reno moved there, 196 people lived in the Chance area. For a short time, the district even had a school. Reno continued to practice law there and, apparently, ran the general store and post office; he never surveyed for a townsite. By World War I, Chance's glory days were over, and the community eventually melted away. The post office closed in 1921, and the store found its way into a nearby cottonwood grove on the south side of the river.

In 1897, Nathan Chance and his neighbors attempted to get the county commissioners to buy his hand-built timber wagon bridge. The commissioners refused the offer and, in 1914, built a steel truss bridge on a different alignment instead (the old wagon bridge piers are still visible in the river). By World War II, the county had condemned the steel bridge and made plans to replace it. A slim budget, however, limited the county commissioners' options. Accordingly, they hired the venerable William P. Roscoe Company to move two spans of the old Yellowstone River bridge at Fallon to southern Carbon County to replace the Chance Bridge and another structure a mile to the north. Ice jams on the Yellowstone during the winter of 1943 had destroyed two spans of the old bridge at Fallon. The Montana Highway Department replaced the Fallon bridge in 1945, leaving the two remaining spans available for use at an alternate location. Roscoe

Chance never amounted to much. After 1946, it was known mainly for its bridge, which was moved to Chance from Fallon, Montana. *MDT.*

obtained the bridge spans and moved them 230 miles west to Chance, where one of those spans, until recently, stood.

Today, there's virtually nothing left of Chance. It's not even a spot on the map. But it is definitely a place with a past important to Montana history. Maybe no big events happened there and nobody famous ever called it home, but to many, it represented opportunity and hopes for a better life. Montana is a composite of places like Chance—locales that don't exist anymore but are important for what they meant to the people who lived there.

# Chapter 6

# HARD WORK BUILDS CHARACTER

## THE EASTSIDE HIGHWAY
## AND CONVICT GRADE

*M*ontana has a rich and varied history of road building. John Mullan built the first engineer-designed road when Montana was still a part of Idaho and Nebraska Territories. The route was constructed to the engineering standards of the time and served miners, freighters and pilgrims before the railroad became the preferred mode of transportation in the territory. Most roads, however, just kind of grew from use. They followed old aboriginal trails and the paths of least resistance. Construction was minimal and mostly involved removing rocks and tree stumps, digging a cut and maybe building a simple log bridge. By the early twentieth century, though, the dawn of the automobile age created a whole new industry in the state: building modern roads that would serve the increasing number of automobiles. The first roadbuilders were county crews made up of men paying off their annual road taxes. It wasn't until the homestead boom and the advent of scientific road-building methods that modern highways appeared here in the second decade of the twentieth century. Ironically, those early modern highways were built by men denied the freedom of the open road.

The first professional Montana road builders were prison convicts. Prison warden Frank Conley began working prisoners on road projects in 1910. He was a firm believer that putting the men to work taught them not only self-respect but also a trade they could use when released from the penitentiary. Conley wrote in the penitentiary's 1909 biennial annual report to the state legislature:

*The direct effect of outdoor life, regular habits, and employment on prisoners cannot be too highly estimated. There in the freedom of the mountains, the petty criminal develops brain and brawn. He does not come under the masterful, watchful eyes of a guard, or shrink under the lash of an overseer. He appreciates kindly and human treatment; he works willingly and with the necessary punch and vim that accompanies beneficial results every day. From the brow of the burglar and the bank robber drops the sweat of honest toil. They get time to reflect upon the futility of their past life; their muscles are developed by steady labor, regular meals, and well-cooked nourishing food in abundance. The horse thief and the cattle rustler wield the pick, the axe, and the shovel as they were to the manor born.*

Importantly, prison labor outside the walls also relieved chronic overcrowding inside the prison at Deer Lodge. Road crews usually consisted of "short-timers" and none convicted of capital offenses or career criminals.

At the program's height in 1917, fully one-third of the men sentenced to the prison worked outside the walls at the prison ranch, the brick factory or on the road crews; 53 percent of the "outside" men worked on the road crews. From 1910 to 1912, they built county roads in the vicinity of the prison in Powell County and a substantial reinforced concrete bridge across the Clark Fork in Deer Lodge.

The 1912 Prison Commission policy not only expanded the program into western and south-central Montana but also served as a source of revenue for the penitentiary—and for Frank Conley. The crews ranged from 100 to 250 men. Conley subdivided them into smaller groups of 50 to 75 men, with each group overseen by 3 guards. The guards weren't armed, but had dogs, and were required to be familiar with road-building techniques and the use of black powder. Escape attempts were few because the alternative was a quick trip back to the overcrowded prison. Those who stuck it out received good conduct credit that reduced their sentences; the recidivism rate for the road crews was low.

The work wasn't easy. It was brutal pick and shovel work in remote areas that required extensive excavation and rock work. The men used compressed air drills and explosives, but those were the only concessions that eased the hard work. Prisoners wore gray uniforms, not stripes. The men lived in tent camps that included a mess tent and showers and were required to take a shower every two days. The food was good—at least as good as what they would get in a boardinghouse or railroad camp. Each camp was provided with musical instruments, up-to-date sheet music and current literature, such as magazines, books and newspapers. Evenings were characterized by impromptu concerts and ball games. If the men worked hard and didn't cause trouble, they became eligible for early parole and, if requested, a letter of reference from Conley.

Conley provided the labor and the guards, but the counties provided the picks, shovels and other equipment necessary to build a road. In addition, the counties paid the transportation costs for sending the convicts to the job site, paid the guards and provided the horse teams used in the construction. The prison also provided fifty cents per day per prisoner for food. The convicts worked eight hours a day. The camps included cooks, "flunkies," a barber and a laundryman. In 1913, around three hundred Montana convicts were available for road work.

The first major convict-built road in Montana was along the east side of Flathead Lake. In March 1912, the State Board of Prison Commissioners implemented a policy that allowed the counties to utilize convict labor for road-building within two hundred miles of the state penitentiary in Deer Lodge. The state (prison) would provide the prisoners' upkeep up to fifty

The prison crews were not chain gangs but organized and motivated laborers who used horses to pull road graders called fresnoes. *MHS Photograph Archives, Helena, 949-980.*

cents a day per man. Anything over that amount was the responsibility of the counties. The counties would provide tents to house the road crews and horses. The counties were also responsible for the black powder, picks, shovels, wagons, scrapers and harness. At first, the counties also paid the salaries of the guards.

In March 1912, the Flathead County Board of Commissioners allocated $10,000 for the construction of a road along the east shore of Flathead Lake. The county was constitutionally bound up to that monetary limit on any one road project. That would prove to be a significant problem for this project. That same month, the county commissioners signed the contract for the use of convict labor. The prison commissioners ordered Warden Conley to send forty to fifty prisoners to "assist in the construction of a public highway on the eastside of Flathead Lake, such road being a portion of the 'Park to Park' Highway."

The proposed East Side Road was the first under the new prison commission policy in 1912; Flathead County was the first to submit an application to use convict road crews. The road would run along the east side of Flathead Lake for twenty-four miles between Bigfork and Polson. That first year, the convicts built a little over six miles of road through some very rugged country. In the process, the project blew through the $10,000 county appropriation by the end of the year with eighteen miles on the project still to go.

The Kalispell Chamber of Commerce managed to raise an additional $5,500 in subscriptions from Flathead County businesses and individuals to keep the project going, but by November 1912, winter weather had stopped construction, and Conley moved the convicts to Sanders County for a project there. Although the county commissioners had signed the contract, they were not happy with its terms, especially that they had to pay the guards too; they felt that the state should pay for the guards.

In December 1912, a delegation from Flathead County, including county commissioner Henry Good (who would later be a highway commissioner), Sheriff A.J. Ingram and county attorney X.K. Stout, appeared before the prison commission to discuss the project. The discussion revolved around the fact that the county had already spent most of its $10,000 appropriation and felt that the state should pay for the guards. It would cost another $12,500, the delegation believed, to finish the project. The prison commissioners didn't agree to the county's request, claiming that other counties had agreed to pay the guards' salaries and it wouldn't be fair to them if they didn't do it in Flathead County too. The convict crews completed work in Sanders

County in July 1913; Conley was ready to send his men back to Flathead County, even though the funding issue hadn't been resolved.

The Flathead County commissioners enlisted the assistance of Senator Fred Whiteside in their disagreement with the prison commission. Whiteside had gained fame in 1899 for blowing the lid off copper king William A. Clark's attempt to bribe Montana legislators into electing him a U.S. senator. Whiteside's colleagues ousted him from the state senate because of the scandal. Whiteside eventually returned to the legislature and served there until 1918. Despite his problems with Clark's cronies, Whiteside was a powerful political force in northwestern Montana.

In late August 1913, Whiteside sent a letter to Governor Sam Stewart after meeting with him at the Lamb's Club in Helena during the legislative session a few months before. He was attempting to obtain a $10,000 appropriation from the legislature to complete construction of the East Shore Road. One of the obstacles Whiteside faced in the legislature was the number of people the road would serve. Only about half a dozen "settlers" lived on the east side of the lake that would benefit from the road. Whiteside claimed the road would not only serve local people but also give Montanans and tourists better access to Flathead Lake and recently established Glacier National Park. Whiteside sold the appropriation based on the fact that the road had recently been designated a "state highway" (although it hadn't) and that it was part of the Park-to-Park Highway (it wasn't). The only stipulation was that the money had to be spent in 1913. Governor Stewart promised to look into the matter.

Conley, in the meantime, wanted to postpone work on the road until 1914. He reasoned that the lake would be frozen over by the time the money became available, making the delivery of supplies difficult. Supplies meant for the road crews were shipped to Somers on a branch of the Great Northern Railway and then carried by boat to the construction site. Conley believed the work would take another four to five months, and he wanted to start work in the spring after the ice left the lake. He didn't get his wish.

Under pressure from Governor Stewart, the prison commissioners agreed to pay the $10,000 out of the general maintenance fund. The governor assured Senator Whiteside that the state would pay for the guards. The county rejoined that the state should pay for everything other than the maintenance of the horses and the prisoners. Whiteside again wrote the governor:

> *Now governor, I am personally responsible for having the prisoners returned here and all of the expense that is not paid by the state must be paid here by individual subscription, as the county cannot legally expend more money*

*on the road, and in fact, the county finances have been in such shape that the commissioners could not appropriate the money for this purpose if they had the legal right to do so. Our Republican friends…giving us the laugh and some of the newspapers say it was only a political trick and the prison board never intended to finish the road and never will do so.…The promise made by the board was widely published here at the time and unless it is fulfilled we democrats are going to be in a hole.*

Despite the financial problems plaguing it, the timing of the project couldn't be better.

The Thirteenth Legislature created the Montana State Highway Commission in March 1913. At its very first meeting, highway commissioners Robert Kneale and A.W. Mahon instructed George Metlen to investigate the possibility of utilizing prison labor to build roads under sponsorship of the commission. After a positive report, the commissioners directed Metlen to work out an agreement with the prison commission and Warden Conley. The counties and the highway commission divided the costs of using the prisoners. The first project that would be overseen by the highway commission utilizing convict labor was the East Shore Road.

With highway commission involvement, Flathead County signed a new agreement with the state in October 1913 for the completion of the road to Polson. The county would still provide the equipment, including pneumatic drills, and feed for the horses. The state would assume all other costs. The work would be done under the direction of highway commissioner George Metlen, and the Flathead County surveyor would establish the centerline.

The following month, the Kalispell Chamber of Commerce began a campaign to raise money through subscription to complete the road. Chamber members met with local citizens and civic clubs to advocate for the road and solicit donations to help construct it. Promoters scattered across the county in their campaign to raise money. At a meeting in Ronan (the state legislature didn't form Lake County until 1923), a chamber spokesman stated:

*This road was undertaken in the first instance at the urgent request of people living along the east shore of the lake who had no way of getting the product of their farms and orchards to market. The settlers came forward with an offer of $7,500, on what was supposed to be one-half the completed highway. The [county commissioners] appropriated an*

*equal amount and work was started. Afterwards the scope of the road was
enlarged and an effort is now being made to construct a highway in such
a manner as to meet the requirement of the commission having the transcontinental highway under construction.*

Work on the road resumed in late October 1913. Conley employed around
111 convicts on the project. They were housed in two camps, one working
south from Yellow Bay and the other working north from somewhere north
of Polson. In March 1914, a convict, Herman Erzinger, was killed when
he stood too close to a black powder explosion. He was halfway through
serving a ten-year sentence for manslaughter. In March 1909, while drunk,
he stabbed to death Fred Bossler, the bartender of the Terrace Saloon in
Billings, because he wouldn't keep the bar open after 1:00 a.m. Erzinger was
the only fatality in a project that used a lot of black powder to blast a road
through the rocks on the east shore of the lake.

The men completed work on the project and opened the road on August
1, 1914. Conley moved the last convict camp the following month to the
Bozeman Pass. The road cost $400 per mile to build for a total cost of $31,825
($825,389 in 2020 dollars). The use of convict labor significantly lowered the
cost of the project. Building the road was way beyond the capability of the
county crews, and there were not, as yet, any professional road contractors in
the state. When it was completed, Warden Conley boasted, "Here a road was
hewn through forests and rocks and a new country opened for development
that would have been neglected for many years had not the state's aid been
available." At 24 miles, it was the longest stretch of highway built by convict
labor in the state. It was also the first convict road built under the auspices
of the state highway commission. It was largely because of this project that
the highway commission assumed all financial responsibilities for the convict
projects and oversaw the construction of nearly 250 miles of road, mostly
through rugged terrain.

At the same time Senator Whiteside was pushing for funds to build the
road in Flathead County, another convict project was about to get underway
in Park County. In July 1912, the Park County commissioners contracted
with Frank Conley to construct four miles of road along the north side of
the Yellowstone River east of Livingston. Conley's contract with the county
required it to provide the convicts with powder, drills, picks, shovels, scrapers,
wagons and horse teams. It also specified that all bridges and culverts built
by the convicts be composed of concrete, with the county providing the
cement. The county surveyor would stake the route and "prepare profiles

of said road showing fills and cuts." The plans specified that the road would measure eighteen to twenty feet wide.

Convicts began work on the road in the spring of 1913. The *Bozeman Republican Courier* reported that month that forty convicts were at work on the road; they were guarded by four men.

> *The road gangsters work, not in stripes, but in ordinary clothing, and their hair is not cropped. The four guards do not make a display of firearms, and about the only significant signs of the camp are the two telephone lines running into the tents of the guards, and connected with the main telephone wires, and the pack of bloodhounds, seven in number, which are kept with the party.*

While at work on the road project, the prisoners lived in a tent camp probably located at the west end of the project near the Shields River. Conley assigned guards to the camp based on their ability to maintain order and discipline. There were no holding cells or manacles in camp, nor the distinctive black-and-white striped uniforms. Prisoners in the road camp wore gray uniforms as they did in Flathead County. Despite the relaxed atmosphere of the work camp, two prisoners attempted to escape. Local authorities picked them up in nearby Big Timber and returned them to the penitentiary in Deer Lodge.

A Park County man named Thompson supervised the work on the road. The *Republican Courier* reported that the men were doing "splendid work with heavy rock construction." Indeed, Conley preferred his captive labor pool to build roads through rocky and hilly terrain rather than the flatlands of eastern Montana because it was more profitable for the prison. The men worked six days a week with Mondays off. They carved a road through four miles of "native rock," including rock cuts eighteen to twenty feet deep. In July 1913, a group of fifty "autoists" from the Bozeman and Livingston automobile clubs toured the newly constructed road "where a mountain hitherto impassable even on horseback had been made into a wide, rock-bottom road of small grade along the Yellowstone…at a cost of $7,000."

Popularly known as the Convict Grade Road by 1914, it was incorporated into the Yellowstone Trail later that year. The trail, a four-thousand-mile interstate highway, connected Plymouth, Massachusetts, and Seattle, Washington. In 1914, the Yellowstone Trail Association met at Hunter's Hot Springs at the eastern terminus of the Convict Grade section. Considerable promotion of the segment occurred because of the method by which it was

Convict Grade was an important and distinctive segment of the Yellowstone Trail for many years. *MDT.*

built and its scenic qualities. The trail association was "very proud of this stretch, and many photographs were taken of the road and the work." The Convict Grade served as part of the federal aid highway system until 1926, when the State Highway Commission rerouted the road to the south side of the Yellowstone River and designated it U.S. Highway 10. The Convict Grade continues to function as a county road.

The Montana State Highway Commission worked in close collaboration with Warden Conley and the counties that sought their services for road projects. Very early in the program, commission member George Metlen realized the limitations of the use of convict labor; cost effectiveness occurred only on projects that involved "heavy rock cuts and timber clearing" because of the high overhead charges for the guards and equipment. By 1915, the commission furnished most of the equipment for the convict crews, including picks, shovels, dump wagons and horse teams. After World War I, however, they became increasingly marginalized in the highway commission's statewide highway program because of the limitations in their use. Indeed, prison road crews worked, for the most part, in western Montana.

Competition between road contractors and the prison crews grew after World War I. That led to complaints to the highway commission by the contractors, who felt the convicts had an unfair advantage. Increasingly during the 1920s, the highway commission used prison crews in more isolated areas doing work that would have been too expensive under contract with private firms. Consequently, the number of convict crews during the decade dwindled. The limitations of the use of that kind of labor also became more apparent to the highway commission and less cost effective to the state. The highway commission terminated the program in 1925.

There are a few places around the state where you can still see the work the convict crews did building Montana's first automobile routes. Convict Grade is listed in the National Register of Historic Places. Their work is prominent on the west side of the Yellowstone River in Yankee Jim Canyon north of Gardiner and on the old I-90 frontage road between Drummond and Clinton. Their legacy has been left in the rocks that they struggled through in an attempt to improve their lives and Montana's transportation system.

Chapter 7

# STANDING TALL

## THE RAINBOW TRANSMISSION LINE

*R*emnants of Montana's industrial past are everywhere to be seen. It's much more than the residue of mining and smelting. And Butte and Anaconda are just part of the story. Much of it isn't much to look at, and in a few places we take it for granted. They certainly represent a different time in Montana's colorful history. A time when mining dominated the state's economy and much of the industrial development was geared toward that industry. Motorists traveling on I-15 at Elk Park north of Butte might notice a line of electrical transmission towers that march across the valley parallel to the interstate. They are also present in the Helena Valley and in the vicinity of Great Falls. Built in the first decade of the twentieth century, the steel towers still carry electricity between Great Falls and Butte. It may be the oldest transmission line still in use in the United States.

Although small electrical plants provided a few Montanans with electricity in the late nineteenth century, the state electrified on an industrial scale in the early twentieth century. Newly completed hydroelectric dams on the upper Missouri River near Great Falls provided electricity to the mines, mills and smelters of Great Falls, Butte and Anaconda. The power generated at the dams was also used for domestic and commercial purposes and provided the motive power for the Milwaukee Road and Butte, Anaconda and Pacific Railroads, along with the Butte public trolley system. Called the Rainbow Transmission

Line, it conveyed electricity from the Rainbow hydroelectric dam at Great Falls to Butte, a distance of 128 miles. The line was erected by the Great Falls Water Power and Townsite Company (GFWPTC) in 1909 and consists of 2,030 steel transmission towers.

Designed by Max Hebgen, the line followed the shortest distance between Rainbow Falls Dam in Great Falls and a substation outside Butte. Work began on erecting the towers on July 28, 1909, and the project was completed on May 20, 1910. Milliken Brothers of Staten Island, New York, fabricated the towers to Hebgen's specifications. Erection of the towers began in Great Falls and moved south to Butte. Each tower weighed about two thousand pounds and cost $133 (about $3,500 in today's dollars) each to install, including footings, assembly and erection.

Hebgen also oversaw the construction of what was popularly known as the Rainbow Line. He employed a maximum of five work crews on the project, ranging in number from twenty to eighty men depending on the type of terrain. The workers assembled the towers on the ground and hoisted the towers into place using a simple crane, called a gin pole. On average, the workers could raise ten towers during a nine-hour shift. On their best day, the men erected twenty-six towers. Each tower carried redundant wires to ensure uninterrupted service in case lightning or vandalism knocked out a line. Testing of the power line began in early June 1910, and it was ready to carry power from Rainbow Falls Dam to Butte two days later. The dam began to provide power to the Butte mines and to the Anaconda smelter by the middle of August 1910. The total cost of the line was $270,152 ($7 million today).

Each forty-two-foot-tall tower carried three six-strand hemp-centered, hard-drawn copper cables manufactured by Roebling and Sons, which also provided the ground wires. From each conductor was suspended a "string of six ten-inch disc insulators, furnished by the Ohio Brass Company. Each disc received a factory test for electrostatic and mechanical defects before shipment." The line utilized 780 miles of copper wire, 520 miles of steel wires and 7,504 ceramic insulators. The original power lines remained in operation until 1960, when the Montana Power Company replaced them. The company, however, didn't replace the insulators, and they are still in use after 107 years. When the line became operational, it was the second power line of this type in North America, the first being the transmission line from Niagara Falls to Toronto.

The generators in Rainbow Falls Dam on the Missouri River at Great Falls produced 6,600 volts of electricity that was boosted to 102,000 volts

*Left*: The Rainbow Transmission Line was one of the first high-tension electrical lines to cross Montana in the early twentieth century. *Kristi Hager Photograph, MDT.*

*Below*: Built in 1910, the transmission towers provided electricity to Butte from the recently rebuilt Rainbow Dam at Great Falls. *Kristi Hager Photograph, MDT.*

and then sent out over the wires to Butte. In Butte, the voltage was stepped down to a level that could be used for the mining and smelting operations and for the city trolley system.

The historic transmission line is easily visible from Interstate 15 and a host of primary and secondary roads between Butte and Great Falls. Most folks take electricity and the delivery systems of it for granted. In the early twentieth century, though, it was a big deal, worthy of note in engineering journals. Even something as simple as a transmission tower can have great historical significance.

# Chapter 8

# MILWAUKEE ROAD
# RAILROAD SUBSTATIONS

*I*t's hard not to notice the large brick buildings standing next to Secondary Highway 294 near Lennep and at Ravenna between Drummond and Missoula along Interstate 90. The Ravenna building is particularly noteworthy because of the decay and the large tree growing out of one of the clearstory windows. But, like the Montana Concrete Company plant mentioned in chapter 10, their exact purpose is often unknown to most motorists. One thing is definite, though: they look out of place on the Montana landscape. They're inconsistent with the wild backdrop outside the urban areas. So what were they? The buildings are an important part of Montana's railroad and industrial history. They harken back to the time when railroads were a driving force behind the state's economy. The buildings are associated with the Chicago, Milwaukee, St. Paul and Pacific (Milwaukee Road) Railroad and represent a significant technological feat in the early twentieth century.

The Milwaukee Road incorporated in Montana in 1905 when company chairman Roswell Miller decided to extend the line through the state to the Pacific coast. Winston Brothers began construction of the line between Butte and Avery, Idaho, in August 1908. The Milwaukee initiated passenger traffic on its western extension in 1909. The Milwaukee was the third line with transcontinental connections to cross the Treasure State. The completion of the railroad through the Treasure State coincided with the inception of the homestead boom. Like the Northern Pacific and Great Northern Railroads, the Milwaukee was responsible for bringing thousands of people to the state to try their hand at farming.

Even before the Milwaukee Road completed its extension westward to the Pacific Ocean in 1909, company president A.J. Earling began laying the groundwork to electrify the line in the Rocky Mountain Division, which encompassed 440 miles between Harlowton, Montana, and Avery, Idaho. Earling, however, conceived of a plan wherein the railroad would provide its own electricity to power its locomotives. General Electric, at Earling's direction, initiated plans regarding the electrification of the railroad. In 1909, however, the Milwaukee Road's board of directors appointed a new member to represent the Pacific extension: John D. Ryan, president of Montana's Anaconda Copper Mining Company (ACM). Ryan expressed considerable interest in the potential of electrifying the railroad based on his experience with the electrified Butte, Anaconda and Pacific Railroad then operating between Butte and Anaconda. Importantly, electrification would require enormous amounts of copper, something the ACM had in abundance. Ryan's interest in electrifying the Milwaukee Road was twofold: it would benefit the ACM, plus he also owned majority interests in the Great Falls Power Company, the Thompson Falls Power Company and power companies in Washington State.

Because of Ryan's experience and influence, he convinced the board of directors of the advantages to the railroad to make arrangements with existing power companies, like the Great Falls and Thompson Falls firms, to provide energy to the Milwaukee Road rather than construct its own power stations. The directors also calculated the cost-effectiveness of electrifying the line over the Rocky Mountains rather than depending on more costly and inefficient steam locomotives with their limited travel ranges and frequent stops necessary to take on fuel and water. The directors believed, rightly, that electrification would lower costs and improve service. Consequently, in 1912, the railroad decided to electrify its line through the Rocky Mountain Division and contracted with the Great Falls Power Company for electricity; the directors made a similar deal with the Thompson Falls Power Company the following year.

The Milwaukee began to electrify the Rocky Mountain Division's 440-mile line in April 1914. Construction involved the installation of 100,000-volt power lines to the substations strung along the line in Montana and Idaho. The line carried a three-phase alternating current (AC) to the substations, where it was stepped down to a 3,000-volt direct current (DC) that was "applied directly to a heavy copper cable paralleling the track…and connected to the trolley on two copper wires…supported over the center of the track about twenty-five feet about the rail and directly feeding the locomotives the energy needed for propulsion by means of a pantograph." By use of a regenerative braking system, locomotive systems recovered about 60 percent of the energy required to pull trains upgrade. The first train using an electric locomotive operated between Three Forks and Deer Lodge in November 1915, with the entire Rocky Mountain Division electrified in 1916. The following year, the Milwaukee's board of directors authorized the electrification of the railroad's line between Othello and Tacoma in Washington State. Electrification proved an unqualified success, making the Milwaukee Road one of the most technologically advanced railroads in the United States.

The Milwaukee Road relied on a series of substations to transform the 100,000-volt AC to a 3,000-volt DC to power the railroad's locomotives. Contrary to popular belief, the substations did not generate electricity for the locomotives. General Electric Company electrical engineer A.H. Armstrong and his staff designed the electrical equipment installed in the substations.

Built in 1915, the Milwaukee Road's Drexel Substation, near the Montana-Idaho border, was the center of a small community. *MHS Photograph Archives, Helena, PAc 80.63.04.*

The railroad ordered the equipment for the stations in November 1914 for delivery in May 1915. Reinier Beeuwkes, also an employee of General Electric, supervised the installation of the equipment. The Milwaukee constructed twenty-two substations, thirteen in Montana and nine in Idaho and Washington. In Montana, the stations were spaced an average of thirty-seven miles apart.

The stations were substantial brick buildings that housed the motor-generator sets and low-tension switching equipment in the front part of the structure and the high-tension transformers and switching equipment in the two-and-a-half-story section of the building. The motor-generator sets converted the AC to DC that fed the locomotives. Substations housed either two or three motor-generator sets, with one functioning as a backup. Lightning arresters and horn gaps sat on the roof of the transformer section and the power lines connected to the building through the motor-generator section. (A horn gap consists of two horn-shaped metal rods separated by a smaller air gap that serves as a lightning arrester. A horn gap usually consists of porcelain insulators that serve to dissipate lightning charges into the ground.) The foundations and roofs of the buildings were reinforced concrete and walls composed of brick. Construction of the two different styles of substations designed and built by the Milwaukee Road depended on location; the majority were flat-roof buildings, while those in areas of heavy snowfall featured gable roofs. Only the substations at Drexel and East Portal in Montana sported gable roofs. Pits to aid in air circulation around the electrical equipment were located below the concrete floors. The large windows "are of steel sash construction and are of liberal dimensions and carefully placed to insure good general illumination"; they also functioned to assist air circulation inside the building.

Electrical power was fed to the substations through electrical connectors on the façade of the operations office portion of the building. The operations office contained the switchboard for the motor-generator sets and also functioned as a ticket office and waiting room, since most substations also served as railroad stations. The extended bay overlooked the track, which enabled the substation operator to "keep in touch with train movements and perform other duties besides those pertinent only to substation operations." Operators manned substations on a twenty-four-hour basis, while operators in more remote locations resided in houses near the station. The operators controlled the voltage to the lines feeding electricity to the locomotives, started and stopped the motor-generator sets and recorded power usage. Originally, locomotives required a minimum of 1,800 volts for power, but that

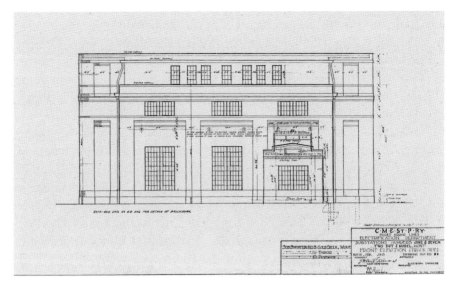

The Milwaukee Road's substations were substantial brick structures bristling with electrical equipment to power the railroad's locomotives. *Author's collection.*

amount increased to 3,200 volts in the 1950s. Milwaukee Road locomotives were supplied with current by more than one substation at a time to ensure continuity of operation. The utility companies supplied the power at about $.0054 per kilowatt hour. Spur tracks from the main line entered the motor-generator room of each substation to allow heavy equipment to be unloaded from railcars with a ten-ton crane positioned inside the building.

In 1948, the Milwaukee Road hired electrical engineer Laurence Wiley to institute low-cost changes to the railroad's Rocky Mountain and Coast divisions (Washington State). In 1950, he devised a method to automate some of the substations and operate them using remote control. Implementing Wiley's idea fell to Milwaukee Road engineer Earl Barnes, who developed the means to achieve the remote-control operations. Tarkio, about forty miles west of the Primrose Substation, and within the Rocky Mountain Division, received the first remote control system. With three substations controllable from one location, the setup allowed the Tarkio operator to control operations at both the Drexel and Primrose stations.

By the late 1960s, the railroad's electrification system required costly upgrades. The trolley wires that carried the electrical current to the locomotives were in good condition, but most of the forty thousand wood poles that carried the wires required replacement. In addition, most of the electric locomotives needed to be replaced. The Milwaukee Road estimated the cost of the upgrade to the system at around $39 million. After considerable debate among the railroad's board members, they decided to scrap the electrified system as too costly and purchased additional diesel locomotives. Milwaukee Road maintenance crews began removing the wires in 1973. The section including the Primrose Substation ceased electric operations in 1974. The railroad sold most of the substations to salvagers, who demolished the buildings. In Montana, only four of the railroad's thirteen Montana substations escaped the wrecking ball: at Loweth west of Lennep in Meagher County, the Gold Creek Substation in Powell County, the Ravenna Station between Missoula and Drummond and the Primrose Substation ten miles west of Missoula.

The Milwaukee Road held the honor as the third and last transcontinental railroad to cross Montana. Established primarily to haul freight, the Milwaukee Road faced declining revenues throughout much of its history in Montana, twice declaring bankruptcy, once in 1925 and again in 1938. Competition from the Northern Pacific and Great Northern Railroads along with cyclical drought and two economic depressions prevented the Milwaukee Road from becoming the cash cow the board of directors envisioned in 1909. After a short boom during the Second World War, the railroad again found itself in dire economic trouble, finally abandoning its lines in Montana in 1980.

Arguably, the best-preserved Milwaukee Road substation is located at the old railroad station of Primrose about ten miles west of Missoula off Mullan Road. Established as a station in 1914 and named for the plant that grew profusely in the area, Primrose Substation No. 10 followed a standard design utilized by Milwaukee Road Railroad architects in Montana, Idaho and Washington. A railroad contractor built the substation out of brick according to the standardized design in 1915. The substation features the flat-roof architectural design embodied by eleven of the thirteen substations in Montana. Operation of the substation began in 1916. The station housed two motor-generator sets and employed three men, each working an eight-hour shift. The men lived on-site with their families. In addition to the substation, the Primrose Substation complex included a water tank, pump house, operator's car body, shed, two residences, an outhouse, tower, coal and oil house, stone house, icehouse, garage and two-story section house. The railroad tracks, ties, ballast and other appurtenances associated with the railroad were removed in the 1980s, although the grade remains. The substation is now owned by a private individual.

# Chapter 9

# LOCAL BOY MAKES GOOD

## JOE STUBKJAER AND HIS AMAZING INVENTION

*A*fter all these years, Montana history still amazes me. Just when you think you've seen it all, something pops up that surprises and astonishes you. The stuff in the history books is interesting enough on its own, but it's the things that you find "out there" that are just as fascinating. Books are great, but being able to see, experience and sometimes touch what historically made Montana the Last Best Place is even better. Nowhere is this better represented than in a nondescript concrete building just south of the railroad tracks at the intersection of Pratten Street and Clough Avenue in Columbus.

At first glance, the building seems rather plain. It is built of sandstone cut from the old Montana Sandstone Company quarry north of town. Stone extracted there in the early twentieth century was used to construct the state capitol building in Helena. After the completion of the capitol, other people, such as Italian immigrant Pasquale Petosa, quarried stone there for buildings and cemetery headstones. Petosa constructed this building at the intersection of Pratten and Clough for local blacksmiths Hans Olson and Joe Stubkjaer in 1913. Petosa's business was located next door to the south. Born in Copenhagen in 1865, Stubkjaer immigrated to the United States in 1892 and arrived in Columbus from South Dakota in about 1910. He and Olsen leased this building as a warehouse to a couple of downtown Columbus merchants and later to John C. Calhoun, a local automobile mechanic. Sandstone buildings are common in Columbus, but it's what's attached to the rear of the building facing onto Pratten Street that's really interesting.

The two concrete buildings at the rear of the warehouse don't seem like much when you look at them, but they both have an important history that involves the United States' most famous inventor, Thomas Alva Edison. In addition to being a blacksmith, Joe Stubkjaer was also an inventor. In 1913, he developed a new way to pour double concrete walls with dead air space between them. The empty space helped remove the dampness characteristic of the interiors of solid concrete-walled buildings. It was an important invention. In order to build a hollow-walled concrete building at that time, walls were poured in sections. As each level set, builders removed the forms for each section and then poured the next layer. It was a slow and laborious process to say the least. Stubkjaer's invention used one large form custom-built with a dead air space in between. Stubkjaer's process resulted in walls that could be poured quickly and finished shortly after the concrete had set and the forms removed. These two seemingly innocuous structures in Columbus that look like bunkers were the first built under Stubkjaer's process. The *Columbus News* encouraged its readers to take a look at the prototypes: "it would be ten minutes well worth the effort."

Stubkjaer and his business partners, Harry Raiff, W.W. Clarke and Hans Olsen, intended to use his invention to build cheap concrete houses. To that end, they formed the Tubular Wall Company in 1914. The company planned to rent or sell Stubkjaer's invention or license the rights to use it. They built at least one demonstration house in Columbus in September of that year and may have built one or two in Billings the following year. The company claimed that it could build a five-bedroom, 57-square-foot house for only $575—without the plumbing. Incredibly, according to the *Harlem Enterprise*, the company could build a house in a day. Stubkjaer claimed the house could be "regarded as a wonder of cheapness and durability." It is

These seeming nondescript buildings in downtown Columbus are the prototypes of Joe Stubkjaer's invention for constructing hollow-walled concrete structures. *Joan Brownell photo, MDT.*

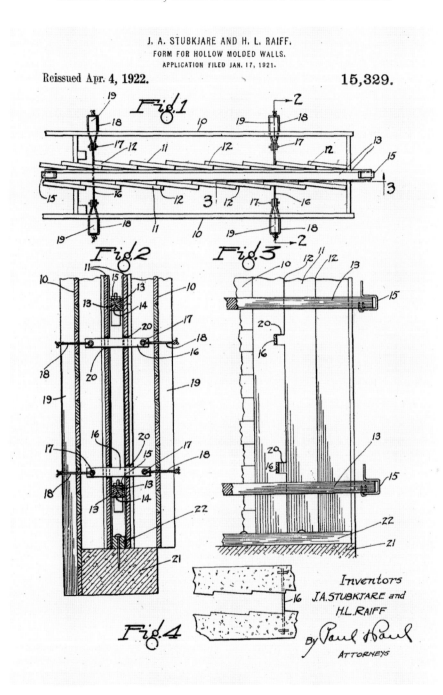

United States patent number 15,329 illustrates the system Joe Stubkjaer invented to construct practical hollow-walled concrete buildings. *U.S. Patent Office.*

not known if the building in Columbus still stands or how many houses the company eventually built.

But before Stubkjaer and his associates began operations, he wrote Thomas Edison a letter to make sure his process didn't infringe on an invention Edison had developed to pour hollow concrete walls a few years before. Unlike Stubkjaer's method, Edison's process required the interior walls to be lathed and plastered "in order to get the advantage of the dead air space." Edison's invention accomplished the same goal as Stubkjaer's, but with none of the time or labor savings. Surprisingly, the competitive Edison wrote back to the blacksmith in the negative, stating that he'd been unsuccessfully working on improving his method since 1909. Joe Stubkjaer had, apparently, out-invented the country's greatest inventor.

The Tubular Wall Company was active into the early 1920s, and the federal government granted the patent for the invention to the company rather than Stubkjaer. It is not known how many buildings the company may have constructed. It is known, though, that Stubkjaer's method was used primarily to build concrete bank vaults. The 1910s was a time of tremendous population growth in eastern Montana because of the 1910–18 homestead boom. Almost every new town had its own bank. In many cases, the bank vaults are all that remains of many once-optimistic communities in the eastern part of the state. The company, however, never filed an annual report with the Montana secretary of state's office and had disappeared by 1930. Joe operated a blacksmith shop in the unit closest to the alley (on the right side of the photograph) until 1928, when he moved to Big Timber. He ran a blacksmith shop there for many years before moving to Shepherd in the late 1930s. He died in Santa Barbara, California, while visiting a daughter in September 1948.

From 1913 to 1928, the sandstone portion of the building and the middle concrete unit functioned as a warehouse for agricultural implements and secondhand furniture. Beginning in October 1928, however, local mechanic John C. Calhoun conducted an automobile repair business in the building. He also sold gasoline from a pump sheltered by a tin roof facing onto Pratten. Calhoun was a descendant of one of Columbus's founding fathers, Patrick Lavelle, and served as an airplane mechanic during World War I. He operated his repair business from this building until retiring in 1960. Calhoun passed away in Columbus at age seventy-four in May 1969.

This seemingly bland building near the railroad tracks possesses a wealth of history important not only to Columbus but to eastern Montana as a whole. Its connection to Thomas Edison is also interesting. It just goes to prove that in sometimes ordinary packages lurk real treasures.

## Chapter 10

# THE MONCRETE PLANT
# IN THE GALLATIN VALLEY

*M*ontana was filled with towns and communities, many of which no longer exist, and their exact locations can sometimes be difficult to pinpoint. They never had enough people living in them to warrant a post office. No surveyor ever filed a townsite plat, and they were so small or active for such a short time that they never made it onto a map. Items appear in local newspapers stating that so-and-so was visiting friends or relatives there, but where "there" was is a mystery. Only a few people ever called them home, and the places have completely disappeared from the landscape. They're not even ghost towns. Sometimes a vestige of the place remains and, over the years, is the subject of speculation. One of those places stands within plain sight of the eastbound lanes of Interstate 90 in Gallatin County. It is the last remnant of a few men's faith in Gallatin County.

About two miles west of Logan, built into the side of a cliff, is a concrete building that is now prominently decorated with graffiti. Except for the graffiti, it nearly blends into the background. The building is all that remains of Dan Morrison's Montana Concrete Company (MCC). The company was active from 1911 to about 1923, when it went into receivership. The MCC manufactured cement building blocks, railroad ties, fence posts, sewer tiles, precast beams, slabs and culverts. The workers and their families lived in nearby Moncrete. Today, all that remains of the operation are gravel storage bins and possibly a small cemetery on top of the bluff behind it.

Dan Morrison came to Montana in 1876 and worked as a foreman at various mines in the southwestern part of the state until 1890, when he formed the Jefferson Lime and Flux Company. Limestone is used to manufacture flux, an important component for processing copper ore. There are plenty of suitable outcrops of limestone in western and southwestern Montana. Morrison's first limestone quarry was located at Lime Spur in the Jefferson River Canyon east of Cardwell. He later sold his interest in that operation and turned his attention to the Gallatin Valley. Morrison is famous today as the discoverer of what is now known as Lewis and Clark Cavern, one of the state's premier attractions. The cavern is located a short distance from Lime Spur. In 1907, he helped establish the Three Forks Portland Cement Company and was involved in the construction of a large processing plant at Trident. By 1911, though, he was looking for new economic opportunities.

The bluffs and cliffs around Trident are composed of Madison limestone that is particularly good for manufacturing lime for cement. When mixed with sand and aggregate, cement creates concrete, which was becoming popular as a building material in Montana in the early twentieth century.

In June 1911, Morrison and partners O.G. Gibson and Charles M. Johnson incorporated the Montana Concrete Company. The company acquired 125 acres and began construction of a plant about four miles southeast of Trident. The Three Forks Portland Cement Company was a key player in the operation since it was heavily invested in the new firm and provided the cement for the manufacture of MCC's products. Indeed, Gibson was the manager of the Portland Cement Company. H.B. Frankenstein of South Bend, Indiana, was the plant superintendent. He was "an expert and specialist in everything pertaining to cement manufacture and kindred machinery." There are few details about what the operation consisted of other than it included four sixty-five-foot-by-ten-foot steam kilns and a drying yard. According to the *Manhattan Record*, the plant could manufacture thirty thousand concrete bricks per day. The operation employed eight men in 1912.

While the location of the MCC is known, the site of Moncrete is a little more problematic. The community sat between the Northern Pacific and Milwaukee Road Railroads, both of which built sidings to the plant. Surveyors never platted a townsite, and it never had a post office. The fact that people once lived there is mentioned in the local newspapers, which regularly ran columns devoted to informing their readers about the comings and goings of the locals. It doesn't appear that Moncrete ever had a school, a voting precinct or even a general store.

The Montana Concrete Company's storage bins built into the side of a cliff have invited speculation for generations of motorists. *Rob Park Photo, MDT.*

The MCC was short-lived. In August 1915, a fire of unknown cause destroyed the company plant, causing $17,000 in damages. Morrison and his partners vowed to rebuild the enterprise. By June 1916, the plant had largely been rebuilt and even expanded. The storage building was part of the operation's expansion. It stored gravel mined from a pit on top of the bluff. The gravel was loaded into railcars from the four apertures on the front of the building. The railroad spur was on the bed of the existing road in front of the building. The gravel was used for aggregate to manufacture concrete.

The *Manhattan Record* reported that a "force of carpenters [had] been busy at the plant for some time past putting in storage bins for gravel and sand which they have been shipping out in large quantities this past spring." The company's owners hired Bozeman architect Pomeroy P. Vreeland to supervise the reconstruction of the plant. His tenure with the company, however, was short-lived when the federal government mobilized the Montana National Guard to go to the Mexican border to hunt down Pancho Villa. Vreeland was a lieutenant in Company A, Second Montana Regiment. It appears that with Vreeland's departure, the rebuilding process stalled. From 1917 to 1923, when the company filed its last annual report with the Montana secretary of state's office, the MCC languished.

After July 1916, there is no hard evidence that the MCC resumed operations. The company went into receivership in 1922, and a lengthy court battle ensued over its debts. The reasons for the business failure are

The massive building contains bins to store gravel mined from a nearby pit. The gravel was used to manufacture concrete products. *Rob Park Photo, MDT.*

unclear, but it may have had something to do with the products. Good cement is based on the quality of the lime, and apparently, the MCC's source was not all that great. The company produced poor-quality materials that were often too heavy. The Continental Oil Company (Conoco) unsuccessfully petitioned the court to be appointed the receiver for the MCC. Judge William E. Carroll denied the request. A month later, in February 1922, John B. Frisbie, representing Conoco, filed suit against the MCC, seeking $23,500, the sale of its property and that the investors' bonds be declared void. That same month, Conoco appealed Judge Carroll's decision to be appointed receiver for the MCC. In May 1922, Justice William Holloway affirmed that "directors of a corporation who permit the company to exceed in indebtedness the amount of capital of the concern, cannot be successfully sued to make good the debts." The company liquidated its assets in 1923.

In a nutshell, in 1916, the Montana Concrete Company built the structure standing next to I-90 to store gravel for the manufacture of concrete. Over the years, all kinds of theories have been posed as to what the building was used for. The facts are interesting enough, but maybe the speculation is more fun. As for Moncrete, it last appears in the newspapers in 1923, and all traces of the community have disappeared.

Chapter 11

# A MONTANA SOAP OPERA

## THE TRIALS AND TRIBULATIONS
## OF PETE GALETTI

*D*espite its quiet setting today, Browns Gulch, about five miles west of Butte, was once a hotbed of activity during Butte's heyday as the World's Greatest Mining Camp. Not only did placer and hard rock mining occur there, but logging, dairying and ranching were also activities on the gulch. During Prohibition, the gulch was infamous for the number of illegal stills there. The Browns Gulch community was big enough to warrant the establishment of a school in 1884. It served local families until closing in 1959. A small stone building at the south end of the project, however, initiated a particularly interesting encounter with Browns Gulch history.

Browns Gulch was one of two dairy centers in the Butte area (the other was in Elk Park). Many of the gulch dairies were operated by ethnic Italians who immigrated to the United States from northern Italy and southern Switzerland. The dairymen, for the most part, got their start in the upper reaches of the gulch harvesting timber for use in the mines on the Butte hill. The dairy industry was important to Butte's existence since it provided fresh milk, eggs, butter and other products to the residents of the city. The dairies were far away from the smoke and soot that settled on the city from the smelters and mills on the Butte Hill. The descendants of many of those original families still live on Browns Gulch.

At the southern end of the gulch, next to a prominent rock outcrop, stands an extensive ranching operation that originated as a dairy and is now owned by a descendant of one of Browns Gulch's early Italian inhabitants. Not only does the ranch display some noteworthy architecture, but it also has a fascinating history that dates back to its original owner, Vettale "Pete" Galetti. He immigrated to the United States from Italy in 1883. By late 1888, Galetti was in the Butte area and worked with other Italian immigrants harvesting timber on upper Browns Gulch. Galetti came to Browns Gulch with a bad reputation. His fellow workers claimed that he had killed two people in Italy and fled to the United States to escape prosecution.

In 1889, Galleti married an eighteen-year-old Italian woman, Gioconda Bersanti, in Butte. The couple had a baby boy a couple months later. In August 1891, Galetti caught his wife in bed with the best man from their wedding. A month later, Galetti again walked in on his wife while she was in *flagrante delicto* with a different man. Galetti filed for divorce from his wife, and the judge granted him full custody of their son. Prior to the divorce, however, Galetti was arrested for attempted murder. He took offense at something said to him by his six-year-old brother-in-law and tried to drown the boy in Browns Gulch Creek. When a bystander attempted to stop him, Galetti allegedly drew a knife and threatened to cut the rescuer "into small pieces."

Galetti was brought to trial in Butte for attempted murder just two days after the incident. The witnesses were all Italians who either did not speak English or did not speak the language well. For some reason or another, the interpreter was not quite up to the task of translating the testimonies. His failings caused considerable quibbling between the prosecution and defense attorneys. The *Anaconda Standard* reporter attending the trial claimed the testimony was "tedious and tiresome." The trial was an uncomfortable one for the spectators as well: "The courtroom was stifling hot, and being packed with a crowd of men whose acquaintance with the bath was remote as to a total stranger, the odor that arose was such as to invite a visit from the Sanitary officer." The trial concluded late that evening. The following day, Judge Muldoon dismissed the charges and released Galetti from custody.

The trial seems to have scared Galetti straight. In 1903, he filed on a 160-acre homestead encompassing a portion of the current ranch. For an unknown reason, however, Galetti built his house, barn and chicken coop on his neighbor's property. When Galetti learned of his mistake, he began moving the buildings onto his land. His neighbor, Zorada Wolfe, sued Galetti to prevent the removal of the structures, claiming she owned them. Galetti had to purchase Wolfe's property to retain ownership of his buildings.

Pete Galetti built this stone house shortly after marrying his second wife. It is reminiscent of the houses in his native northern Italy. *Kristi Hager photo, MDT.*

After fixing that problem, things began to look up for Galetti and his new family—at least for a time. In 1909, he built a new family home. The architectural style was based on similar designs in his native northern Italy near the Alps. As his family and business grew, so did the number of buildings on his property. Eventually, it included two substantial houses, one for him and his wife and the other for his son and his family. It also boasted a granary, a garage and a sizeable bunkhouse—all of which were built of stone. Galetti sold his dairy products in Butte under the name Sanitary Dairy, delivering to homes and businesses throughout the Mining City.

Although Galetti put his checkered past behind him, trouble found him again in 1927. In April of that year, a ranch hand, Red Allen, and two teenage boys overindulged in moonshine manufactured on Browns Gulch, grabbed a rifle and began to shoot up Galetti's buildings. While Galetti and his wife cowered in a corner of their kitchen, "leaden pellets whizzed through an adjoining room." Allen and his companions advanced toward their home and paid particular attention to the garage. Eventually, the trio left and were later captured by law officers. It is not known why the trio picked the Galettis to pick on.

Pete Galetti operated the dairy until he died of a stroke in 1929. Ownership of the property then passed to his widow after a decade-long fight in probate court. His son Marcellino and grandson James operated the dairy until the 1950s. James closed the dairy to concentrate on cattle ranching. A descendant of Galletti's operates the ranch today.

You never know where history will take you. One plain stone building next to a state secondary highway reveals a wealth of mayhem, adultery, attempted murder and, ultimately, triumph. Who says history is boring?

## Chapter 12

# MONUMENT TO A FALLEN ANGEL

About a mile south of Havre on Beaver Creek Road (Secondary 234) stands a lonely stone chimney on the east side of the road. It looks out of place when compared to the flat tabletop nature of the landscape around it. Like other roadside monuments, it generates a lot of speculation by those who pass by it on the way to Beaver Creek Park, the largest county park in the United States. The chimney and hearth are associated with the colorful life and tragic death of a famed minister in Havre in the early twentieth century.

Leonard Jacob Christler was born in the Finger Lakes region of New York in late November 1876. He received his spiritual education at St. Andrews Seminary in Syracuse, New York, and was ordained in 1896. After serving for several years as the rector at Calvary Episcopal Church in Homer, New York, Christler was the curate of St. Peter's Church in Auburn, New York, until 1907. That year, his superior, John Brainard, sent him west as the missionary of the Milk River Valley country in northern Montana. His parish, based in Havre, included the vast territory north of the Missouri River from Glacier National Park east to the North Dakota state line. An "aggressive" and "militant" clergyman, he made the rounds on the high line, establishing St. Mathew's Church in Glasgow and Trinity Church in Gildford and laying the foundations for parishes in Malta and another twenty-five communities in northern Montana. He also built the imposing St. Mark's Episcopal Church in Havre in 1918. A dedicated horticulturist, he tended the flowers and shrubs on the church grounds for several years.

He rented a home about three blocks south of the church at 813 Third Avenue. He also maintained a small dryland farm a few miles south of Havre, which he christened Hill Crest or Hill Top Farm.

In addition to his ministerial work, Christler also found time to run for and win a seat in the Montana House of Representatives in November 1909. He served just one term in the House but introduced meaningful progressive legislation aimed at the reform of wayward women and girls and preventing husbands from living off the earnings of their wives if they were employed as prostitutes. Christler was also instrumental in the establishment of the Montana Bureau of Agriculture, Labor and Publicity, an agency that promoted Montana's economic opportunities. Newspaper accounts suggest the reverend was a popular and much-in-demand presence in Montana during his tenure here. He made the rounds of his enormous parish during the height of the homestead boom at least once a month. Christler also took the time to edit the *Montana Citizen*, a Democratic weekly newspaper based in Glasgow. Within a short time, Reverend Christler had gained a statewide and national reputation. Shortly after his death, the *Glasgow Courier* wrote:

Leonard J. Christler's popular sermons and lectures earned him the title the "Bishop of All Outdoors." But that popularity hid a dark side. *MHS Photograph Archives, Helena, Stout 2 p.640a.*

> As the result of the diversity and bigness of the work in the Milk River Valley Mission field and because of Rev. Christler's every day practical application of the Kingdom of God, to the needs of all sorts of conditions of men, he had been styled the "Bishop of All-Out-Doors [sic]" by those among whom he has ministered for fourteen years. Montana, the Land of Majestic Shining Mountains and the "Bishop of All Outdoors" are synonymous terms.

The good reverend also wrote articles for national magazines on dryland farming on the northern Great Plains. Definitely a type-A personality, Christler seemed to know everyone and be involved in everything in northern Montana. A handsome and charismatic man, he was a much sought-after lecturer on religious subjects throughout the state. Christler was a freemason and a member of the Benevolent Brotherhood of Elks, the Fraternal Order of Eagles, the Knights of Pythias and the Independent Order of Foresters, among other civic organizations.

Christler's second home, Hill Crest Farm, was a place where he could get away to relax. The farm was a popular gathering place for the reverend's friends but seemed beset by bad karma. Christler barely escaped with his life and lost a world-class library in an early morning fire in March 1910. A faulty chimney flue caused the conflagration that burned the house to the ground. Christler rebuilt the house, but it burned down again in November 1912. The second blaze was caused by arson. The *Culbertson Searchlight* opined that although the fire didn't represent a big investment on Christler's part, it did "represent his savings for several years and many days of hard personal labor that he put in to fix up as attractive abode for himself and the entertainment of his visiting friends, and they were not a few in the course of the year." Fortunately, Christler was in eastern Montana when the second fire occurred. The *Searchlight* claimed the authorities knew who set the fire. Local gossip, though, suggested that it may have been torched by a disgruntled female admirer of the Bishop of All Outdoors or by a member of his congregation. No one was ever charged with the crime.

In October 1914, Leonard Christler married Anna Wadsworth, the daughter of scythe manufacturer David Wadsworth, in Auburn, New York, his hometown. There were, however, some questions about his motives in the marriage. He was handsome and outgoing, a popular speaker and had the unique ability of filling the pews of whatever church he was preaching at every Sunday (although one pundit claimed that most of his flock were young women and not all were Episcopalians). Anna, on the other hand, was introverted, somewhat plain and wore black as if in permanent mourning. The couple settled in the house of Third Avenue in Havre, where Leonard resumed his duties as the "Bishop of All Outdoors." She kept to the shadows, content to remain in the background.

During the eight years of their marriage, much was published in Montana newspapers about Christler's activities. In addition to his enormous parish in north-central Montana, he was also a popular speaker, writer and, significantly, lecturer on the Chautauqua circuit. It was largely through his many articles and his personality that he gained a national reputation, based largely on a flattering article written about him by popular author Stewart Edward White. It was White who christened Christler the Bishop of All Outdoors because of his enormous northern Montana parish.

Christler also remained a popular presence in Havre, particularly with the city's female population.

In October 1917, Helena attorney Frank Carleton opened a law office in Havre with Joe Donnelly. With him came his wife, Margaret, and six-year-old stepdaughter, Catherine. Born in Helena in 1889, Margaret Carleton was the granddaughter of prominent Anaconda physician J.M. Sligh and the daughter of mining entrepreneur Donald Davenport. Described as "pretty, vivacious and of particularly jolly disposition," Margaret was everything Anna Christler was not. In 1908, Margaret married hardware store clerk Charles Lotz. The marriage didn't last, and she divorced him in June 1912. She then married Frank Carleton, a rising star in Montana's judicial system, in 1917. Frank adopted Catherine and was, by many accounts, a doting stepfather. After moving to Havre, Margaret quickly immersed herself in the city's society circle, especially after her husband obtained an appointment to the Eleventh Judicial District in 1920. By 1921, though, the couple had separated. On the surface, Margaret blamed the breakup on marital and financial issues. Carleton blamed it on his wife's relationship with Leonard Christler. Frank left Havre for Los Angeles and took Catherine with him.

Soon after the couple separated, Margaret accepted employment with the Midwest Lyceum Bureau, a Chautauqua company based in Chicago. Chautauquas were popular summer entertainment for Americans in the Midwest and West in the late nineteenth and early twentieth centuries. Chautauquas featured inspirational lectures and talks about current events, travel and amusing stories. Musicians, preachers and other entertainers provided programs for the audiences. Christler obtained employment with the same Chautauqua company and toured the country with Margaret in the summer of 1921. In 1922, both worked for the Mutual-Elwell Chautauqua Bureau. Shortly after concluding that summer's tour, Margaret became withdrawn and troubled. Evidence suggests that Leonard may have ended the relationship.

The situation came to a head on October 28, 1922. After an evening out with friends, Leonard and Anna returned home a little after midnight. Margaret arrived at the house in a muddled state about forty minutes later. Despite the late hour, she demanded to talk to Reverend Christler and forced her way into the house. With Anna standing by, Margaret once again professed her love for Christler and told Anna that there was no room for her in his life. Margaret was clearly not in her right mind. Leonard turned to go bed, and at that point, according to the official record, Margaret pulled a small handgun out of her purse and shot the Bishop of All Outdoors through the heart and then turned the gun on herself. It happened so quickly, according to Anna, that she couldn't do anything to prevent the tragedy. She then called doctors Carl Foss and Stuart MacKenzie to the house. After they arrived at the scene, they called the police. The unpleasant incident couldn't help but be sensational, and it did, indeed, generate lurid headlines in Montana and national newspapers.

The coroner's inquest held the day after the shooting eventually concluded that Margaret Carleton murdered Leonard J. Christler and then committed suicide. It was clear from the questioning by jury foreman Raleigh Lindbarger and Hill County attorney Max Kuhr that it was not so clear-cut a conclusion. Since Anna Christler was the only witness to the incident, she spent considerable time on the witness stand. She stated, simply, that Margaret arrived at their home, was agitated about something and then shot her husband and then herself. The men, however, brought other witnesses to the stand to testify about Margaret's state of mind the days and hours prior to the tragedy. Because of her addled state and mumbled speech, Lindbarger suggested she may have been over-medicated on the drugs found in her hotel room and may, indeed, have attempted suicide the day before the incident, as stated at the inquest. Lindbarger's line of questioning intimated that Margaret had had an abortion and that led to the suicide attempt. He questioned Dr. MacKenzie if Margaret, in that state of mind and suffering the aftereffects of trying to take her own life, could have shot Christler with the degree of accuracy shown on his body and then on herself. All knew there was something more to the relationship between Christler and Carleton than what many city officials were willing to testify. Yet the verdict was still murder-suicide. A coverup to protect Havre's most prominent citizen and his socially prominent wife? Likely so, but Lindbarger and Kuhr were unable to conclusively prove it.

Eventually, the sensation died down, and the Bishop of All Outdoors was buried in his hometown of Auburn, New York. Margaret was buried in the family plot at the Forestvale Cemetery in Helena. Frank died in Riverside, California, in June 1960. As late as the early 1990s, somebody placed flowers on Margaret's grave on Memorial Day each year. Anna Christler was a common sight in Havre until just before her death in Auburn in 1942. She spent summers in Havre and tended her husband's beloved flowers at St. Mark's Church. Anna also frequently traveled around the state and lectured at Episcopalian functions, carrying on her husband's legacy. She refused to speak about the incident that claimed her husband's life.

Christler's home twice fell victim to fire. It burned down a final time years after his death, leaving only the chimney. *Kristi Hager photo, MDT.*

As for the Hill Crest Farm south of town: it once again, and for the last time, burned to the ground sometime after Reverend Christler's death. The cause of the fire was not determined but may have been accidental, as it was a popular gathering spot for Havre's teenagers. One story goes that Christler heated the house by a natural gas well drilled on the property. Teenagers liked to drop lighted matches down the pipe to watch the flames shoot up out of the ground. One of those party activities may have gotten out of control and burned down the house. No one will ever know, but the chimney still stands sentinel next to the highway south of Havre—perhaps a testimonial to a mercurial and nearly forgotten Montanan with some very definite human weaknesses.

# Chapter 13

# PUFFS OF GRAY ON THE HORIZON

## THE SNOWDEN AND WOLF POINT BRIDGES

*Approaching Wolf Point from the north, the motorist sees at a considerable distance from the city the three puffs of gray against the darker background of hills beyond. Like miniature clouds of smoke, they seem at first, but unlike either smoke or clouds, they are seen at each succeeding height in the road to be unchanged in shape. A traveler may wonder at the unvarying shape of the pale forms, but to the native of this part of Montana, there comes a thrill as he exclaims: "The Wolf Point Bridge!" Seen at a distance of 15 miles this massive structure appears as vaporous as the ethereal substance of which dreams are made. And it is a dream, a dream that came true.*
—Great Falls Tribune, *June 14, 1930*

𝓑 ig bridges were once a big deal. A bridge could not only open up a community to trade from the surrounding area, but it also branded it as a place do business and a prosperous place to live. Montana history is full of stories about how a bridge promoted the permanence and stability of communities throughout the Treasure State. The Missouri and Yellowstone Rivers in eastern Montana could be daunting obstacles and marginalized the development of many communities along their lengths. Unless you could tap into the enormous areas north and south of the rivers, your town wasn't going anywhere. Consequently, there was a push in the early twentieth century to build big bridges to encourage economic and political development of a region. Two bridges, near Fairview and outside Wolf Point, had particularly significant impacts to the development of northeastern Montana—one because it was a one-of-a-kind structure and the other because it opened the region to development and made Wolf Point an even more important trading center.

The Snowden Bridge is a steel monument rising above the Great Plains of eastern Montana. The state's only vertical-lift bridge, it spans the Missouri River about twelve miles north of the community of Fairview near the North Dakota border. The Snowden Bridge was an engineering marvel of its day, a superstar built during the height of the golden age of steel truss bridge construction in Montana between 1887 and 1921. Until the interstate highway era, the 3,257-foot Snowden Bridge was the state's most massive steel bridge and, for a short time, the longest vertical life span in the world. Today, it has the distinction of being perhaps the most photographed bridge in the state.

Built in 1913, the four-span bridge's design is unpretentious. It consists simply of two 100-foot steel towers supporting a 296-foot vertical lift span. The bridge was constructed so that concrete counterweights in each tower raised and lowered the span, acting much as sash weights do in old double-hung windows. To raise the lift span, a man sitting in the machinery house at the top of the lift span lowered concrete counterweights hanging in the lift towers; the weight of the descent of the concrete blocks raised the lift span. A three-cylinder, kerosene-fueled engine in the machinery house on top of the lift span slowed the descent of the counterweights to control the rate of the span's upward movement. The engine was also used to lower the span back into place by returning the 350-ton counterweights to their original positions. Shipping on the Missouri River in Montana did not warrant the raising of the lift span very often, but when it did happen, it took about thirty minutes to raise the span eighty-four feet to allow passage of the boat.

The Snowden Bridge is a monument to a failed dream: Great Northern Railway president James J. Hill's plan to construct the Montana Eastern Railway from New Rockford, North Dakota, to Lewistown, Montana. During the height of the homestead boom, Hill intended the railroad to supply homesteaders streaming into central and eastern Montana and to ship their agricultural products to markets in the Midwest and eastern United States. The Union Bridge and Construction Company of Kansas City, Missouri, began construction of the Snowden Bridge in late 1912 and completed it by December 1913 at a cost of nearly half a million dollars. The bridge is named for a station on the Great Northern Railway's nearby main line.

Built in 1913 for the Great Northern Railway, the Snowden Bridge, for a time, featured the longest vertical lift span in the world. *MDT.*

In 1916, Hill scrapped his plans to complete the Montana Eastern Railway, and the Snowden Bridge functioned as part of a branch line between Sidney and the Great Northern's Snowden station. Because it was the only river crossing for fifty miles between Williston, North Dakota, and Culbertson, Montana, the railroad outfitted the bridge for vehicular traffic as well as train use in 1926. From 1926 until the mid-1950s, the railroad charged motorists tolls to use the bridge. For years, a tollkeeper collected money from motorists wishing to use the bridge. A motorist had to pay attention though: trains still used the bridge as well.

The Snowden Bridge's lift span was rarely used. During the construction of Fort Peck Dam in the 1930s, loaded barges traveled under the bridge, but the railroad seldom undertook the cumbersome task of raising the span to give them clearance. Instead, barges took on water, lowering their height, in order to pass underneath the bridge. In all, the span was not raised more than sixteen times, the last in 1935. The Great Northern retired the lift machinery and secured the lift span in 1943, but until the 1990s, the lift house with its equipment remained intact atop the center span. The railroad and motor vehicles shared use of the bridge until the 1950s, when the Montana and North Dakota highway departments opened a new bridge across the Missouri River a few miles downstream of the Snowden Bridge.

Before the completion of the Wolf Point Bridge in 1930, residents of northeastern Montana had no reliable or safe way to cross the Missouri River there. Instead, they relied on inadequate ferries and, for a time, a pontoon bridge. During the winter months, farmers and ranchers on the south side of the river had to cross the ice. High water in the spring and early summer rendered the river impassable. After the drowning deaths of two McCone County teenagers crossing the ice at night in February 1926, the Wolf Point Commercial Club, led by county commissioner William L. Young and McCone County commissioner Thomas Horsford, launched a successful campaign to convince the Montana State Highway Commission to build a bridge near the community. The structure, when completed, was an object of intense civic pride not only to Wolf Point but also to the tiny ranching and farming communities in the region. When it was dedicated on July 9, 1930, the *Wolf Point Herald* called the bridge "a memorial to those whose lives have been lost in the Missouri and a monument to those whose co-operation…made it possible."

After lobbying by Young, Horsford and others, Montana representative Scott Leavitt introduced House Resolution 13067 in Congress in May 1926 to provide for the construction of a bridge over the Missouri River at or near Wolf Point. On December 22, North Dakota representative Olger Burtness of the House Committee on Interstate and Foreign Commerce endorsed the bill and forwarded it on to the Senate Committee on Commerce. Committee member David Stewart of Iowa presented the bill to the Senate, where it passed with no dissenting votes on January 11, 1927. President Calvin Coolidge signed the bill authorizing the construction of the bridge three days later.

For a project of this magnitude, the time between approval of the bridge and actual construction was a long one. Funding and debates over the design of the bridge were the main issues of the parties involved. The funding was finally resolved in May 1927. Because the north half of the bridge was within the Fort Peck Reservation, the federal government shouldered 100 percent of the cost for half the bridge. The county commissioners also raised money through bond elections in Roosevelt and McCone Counties. The Great Northern Railway also assumed some of the cost of the bridge, as did the highway commission. With funding secured, the next big obstacle was the design of the structure.

The highway commission and the Bureau of Public Roads settled on a Pennsylvania through truss design for the structure. Then began two years of back-and-forth debate between the two agencies on the nuances of the design. The commission developed a preliminary plan for the bridge that it submitted to the U.S. Corps of Engineers for its approval (the Missouri was classified as navigable in that section of the river). The commission raised the profile of the bridge to accommodate high-water events. Finally, on December 18, 1928, the commission awarded the project to the only company that bid on it: the Missouri Valley Bridge and Iron Company (MVBIC) of Leavenworth, Kansas, for its low bid of $427,644. The company began work on the project in March 1929.

For eighteen months in 1929 and 1930, the Wolf Point Bridge construction site was the most popular tourist attraction in northeastern Montana. In early June, the *Wolf Point Herald* stated that the "bridge site has become a mecca for motorists and picnic parties." Indeed, on October 6, 1929, the site was visited by five hundred people from the Wolf Point area. Visitors included families, state and Great Northern Railway officials and, in one case, "about a dozen cars of members of Hinsdale society." The Wolf Point Commercial Club advertised the bridge as a picnic spot by capitalizing on the community's pride in the partly completed structure.

MVBIC began the task of constructing the bridge's superstructure in mid-November 1929. Highway commission engineer P.M. Hegdal told the *Wolf Point Herald*, "From now on…we will erect, rivet, and swing the trusses into place." Crews accomplished the work with four stationary hoists and an erection hoist mounted on a railcar that traversed the work bridge. The MVBIC fabricated the steel at its Leavenworth factory. From there, the railroad transported the steel to the construction site in nineteen shipments from early September 1929 to late January 1930. Laborers offloaded the 1,150 tons of structural steel at the nearby Macon siding and moved it to the construction site by locomotives borrowed from the Great Northern. The company completed the erection of the two 275-foot steel trusses on January 10, 1930; it completed the massive 400-foot span in mid-February 1930. The company employed around one hundred workers to construct the three truss spans and the two steel girder approach spans.

With the superstructure completed, work crews began laying the reinforcing steel for the deck in May 1930. By the end of the month, the concrete deck had cured sufficiently to allow automobiles to use the bridge. Wolf Point resident Earl Chamberlain was the first to cross the bridge by automobile. Within days, the bridge was regularly used by "southsiders" for access to Wolf Point and the railroad station. By June 22, a Wolf Point businessman had counted 220 vehicles on the bridge during two ten-hour periods. Although the bridge was already opened for traffic and the MVBIC dismantling its construction camp, the city of Wolf Point and, indeed, northeastern Montana enthusiastically firmed up their plans for the bridge's dedication planned for July 9.

Planning for the dedication festivities for the bridge began in early April 1930. First State Bank of Wolf Point cashier Fred Rathert chaired the Bridge Day Committee in charge of organizing the bridge dedication festivities. By June 20, Rathert and his committee announced that the bridge dedication celebration would include five bands, several "distinguished speakers" and, importantly, a daylight fireworks display. Rathert promised that the festivities would be broadcast live on Wolf Point's new radio station, KGCX. Wolf Point native Vera Smith won a contest to lead the planned parade and cut the ribbon officially opening the bridge. The newspaper described the twenty-year-old nurse trainee as having "commingled in her veins the blood of both the Indian and white races. She is a true daughter of the West." With the completion of the bridge on July 1, 1930, the heightened anticipation for the fête was reflected in the increased space given the impending event in the local newspaper.

By midday on July 9, between 10,000 and 15,000 spectators crowded around the Wolf Point Bridge. The crowd, which included 2,500 to 3,000 automobiles, came from as far away as Havre, Minot, North Dakota, and Regina, Saskatchewan. As American flags fluttered from each of the three through truss spans, four airplanes circled over the new structure and the "Indian village" located on the site of the former construction camp. A little after 1:00 p.m., Vera Smith led off the parade from the southern end of the newly christened bridge. In addition to local celebrities, the parade included five bands (including the famed Cowboy Band from Terry) and a float from nearby Vida. The float consisted of a miniature representation of the bridge with agricultural scenes placed in each of the spans and "pretty girls showering the crowd with confetti." The cavalcade also included cowboys, cowgirls, Indians and various forms of antique and modern transportation. Within thirty minutes, the procession had passed over the bridge, and the structure officially opened for traffic.

From a platform under the northern span of the bridge, Wolf Point lawyer and mayor H.N. Marron introduced William Young as the master of ceremonies for ensuing events. After making a short speech, Young presented Montana governor John E. Erickson, who stated that the bridge

The dedication of the Wolf Point Bridge in 1930 was cause for celebration, drawing thousands of spectators from the region. *MHS Photograph Archives, Helena, PAc 2013-50.*

was more than merely a bridge, "for it represents the triumph of the pioneering spirit which must still prevail in Montana if the commonwealth is to occupy its destined place in the Union." Other speakers included Montana Highway Commission chairman O.S. Warden, McCone County commissioner and bridge proponent Thomas Horsford, Saskatchewan chief highway engineer H.R. McKenzie, Great Northern Railway Company president Ralph Budd and, finally, Representative Scott Leavitt. Leavitt recounted the history of the project and, since it was an election year, boasted about his important role in ensuring the construction of the bridge. At the conclusion of the speeches, the bridge was blessed by elders from the Sioux and Assiniboine tribes. The day's official festivities were concluded with a spectacular daylight fireworks display.

The completion of the bridge was a major event for the people of Wolf Point and northeastern Montana, one that was recognized and appreciated by the area's inhabitants. It was the result of many years of active lobbying by William Young and Thomas Horsford that eventually included Montana's congressional delegation. After construction of the bridge had begun, the *Wolf Point Herald* closely monitored its progress and encouraged its readership to vigorously support and promote the project. When completed, the opening of the bridge was a major economic and social event for the community. The *Herald* proclaimed shortly after the dedication that it was "doubtful whether since the coming of the Great Northern Railroad in 1887 that northeastern Montana has given itself to a festival where there has been so much sincere rejoicing and which has such vast significance in the history of our area that aspires to its destined progress."

The Wolf Point Bridge is still the most massive steel truss bridge in Montana at 1,074 feet in length. The 440-foot main span is the longest truss span in the state. It is listed in the National Register of Historic Places and is popularly known as the Lewis and Clark Bridge. Both the Snowden and Wolf Point bridges are testimonials to the optimism their designers, builders and promoters had in Montana.

Chapter 14

# MOTORING THROUGH PARADISE

## THE VIGILANTE TRAIL

**M**otoring was an adventure in the early twentieth century, and people usually didn't travel very far from home. Most roads were choked with dust during the summers, knee-deep in mud in the rainy seasons and blocked by snowdrifts in the winters; road maintenance was minimal year-round. But as more people bought cars, they demanded better roads. Some banded together and formed organizations, like the Good Roads Movement, to advocate for better highways. Those organizations dedicated themselves to the construction of modern roads, which they believed increased commerce and made for thriving communities. One path to prosperity was through tourism. Tourists stayed in local hotels or auto camps, ate at local restaurants and spent money in local businesses. For many communities, like West Yellowstone and Ennis, a good road was just as important as, if not more than, a railroad.

By the mid-1910s, many out-of-state and local promoters had established road associations to designate and publicize roads that connected important tourist attractions, like Yellowstone and Glacier National Parks. The auto associations gave the routes imaginative names, like Yellowstone Trail, Park-to-Park Highway, Electric Highway and Theodore Roosevelt International Highway. In Montana, the roads mainly connected Yellowstone and Glacier National Parks, with "laterals" to other important attractions like the Little Bighorn Battlefield. By 1925, fourteen "named" highways crisscrossed the Treasure State, each with its own colorful symbols that blazed the way.

In 1919, businessmen and promoters in Madison, Jefferson and Silver Bow Counties banded together to form the Vigilante Trail Association, one of the last such road organizations formed in Montana. The trail, which conjured images of stalwart pioneers battling despicable road agents in Montana's mining camps, provided a 150-mile connection between West Yellowstone and Butte. The Vigilante Trail was marked by a round red, white and blue shield with the dreaded vigilante symbol 3-7-77 featured prominently in the middle. The route passed through country steeped in Montana's early history, including Virginia City and Alder Gulch. The road also grazed some of Montana's best fisheries, including the Madison River, "the fisherman's paradise of the West."

The trail's promoters even came up with a little ditty to help lure visitors to southwestern Montana:

> *Follow the Vigilante Trail*
> *That winds like a snail*
> *Thro the playgrounds of the West*
> *The mountains so white*
> *Loom up in the night*
> *And the soft wind lulls you to rest.*

Despite the tranquility hinted at by the rhyme, the promoters specifically hailed the road as "the most historic road in Montana" and made much of its brutal past. The trail association specifically publicized the conflict between the road agents and the vigilantes as the big draw of the trail, directing motorists to visit "romantic and quaint" Virginia City and Robbers' Roost at Laurin. Only passing mention was made of the devastation caused by the gold dredges to Alder Gulch.

Improvements to the route were, at first, the responsibility of the counties it traversed. In 1922, the trail became eligible for federal aid as part of Montana's Seven Percent System under the Federal Aid Road Act. Despite that advantage, the Montana Highway Department had little money to spend on the route during the lean years of the 1920s. In fact, it may have been during novelist Hoffman Birney's trip to the area in 1928 while researching his book *Vigilantes!* that he later wrote:

> *The roads of Montana are, I believe, the poorest of any state in the Union. Even the glorious scenery of the Rockies can't entirely make up for ruts, chug-holes, mud and detours—to say nothing of broken springs*

A landmark on the Vigilante Trail, Robbers' Roost had no connection to the Alder Gulch vigilantes or the road agents they pursued. *Author's collection.*

> *or stone-bruised tires. I turned off the highway some twenty miles from West Yellowstone, heading northward across Reynolds* [sic] *Pass toward Ennis, Montana, and Virginia City, my goal. The road was atrocious, the scenery superb.*

Indeed, frequent road condition reports in the Butte *Montana Standard* described the Vigilante Trail as dusty, badly rutted or not recommended for traffic at all. The Montana Highway Department began improving the road in 1933; it wasn't paved until 1941. By then, however, the Vigilante Trail, like the other named highways, had mostly faded from history. Today, the route of the Vigilante Trail is U.S. 287 to Ennis then Montana 287 through Virginia City to Twin Bridges, where it connects with Montana 41. It terminates a few miles west of Whitehall on old U.S. Highway 10. The historic sites touted by the Vigilante Trail Association remain, and the road, to echo Hoffman Birney, is superb!

# Chapter 15

# THE JEFFERSON CANYON HIGHWAY AND MOUNTAIN VIEW HOTEL

*T*he Roaring Twenties was kind of a mixed bag for Montana and the Montana State Highway Commission. On the plus side, the federal government enacted the Federal Aid Highway Act of 1921, which had a profound impact on Montana. The legislation established limits on the mileage of roads in each state on which federal money could be spent to accelerate the development of a national interstate highway system. To fund the system, the federal government provided the bulk of the money, which had to be matched by the states on a percentage basis. The states raised the matching funds either through bonding (which Montana did not do) or by gasoline and license taxes. Federal allocations to the states were based on population and the amount of public lands within their borders. What Montana lacked in population, it made up for in public lands. Montana could potentially secure enormous amounts of federal funds if it could raise the requisite matching money.

But that's not what happened. While the state legislature enacted a gasoline tax in 1921, most of the money raised by it went directly to the counties instead of the Montana Highway Commission. The commission got only a small percentage of the tax revenue—not enough to match federal funds. Between 1923 and 1925, the legislature took increasingly more of the commission's share and gave it to the counties. It got so bad by 1925 that Montana had to return federal money because it could not raise the necessary match. Montana was the only state to return federal funds. The lack of money nearly ended the road program in Montana. It was not long

Completed in 1930, the Jefferson Canyon Highway was one of the most scenic in Montana, providing access to Lewis and Clark Cavern. *MDT.*

before Montana reputedly had the worst roads in the United States. Help was on the way, however.

In November 1926, Montana voters passed Initiative No. 31, the Good Roads Law, which enacted a three-cents-per-gallon gasoline tax. Revenue from the tax went directly into the State Highway Fund, which the highway commission used to match federal aid highway funds. The passage of the referendum marked a significant change in how the highway commission functioned, as it removed the counties from the funding and planning process. The commission began funding projects under the Good Roads Law in March 1927. The new law also enabled the highway commissioners to look at long-range projects that meshed with the federal government's desire to create an interstate highway system. Improvements to U.S. Highway 10 (formerly the Yellowstone Trail), the primary east–west route through Montana, were a priority for the Montana highway commission.

The new "Big Picture" policy followed by the highway commission was not without controversy. In February 1927, highway department engineers and the commissioners discussed a plan proposed by Jefferson County promoters to reroute U.S. Highway 10 through the Jefferson River Canyon, thereby bypassing the old Yellowstone Trail route between Willow Creek, Harrison and Cardwell. The proposed route, while more expensive to build and maintain, provided a more direct connection between Whitehall and Three Forks. It also took advantage of the proximity of Lewis and Clark Cavern by providing better access to the natural wonder for tourists. The highway commissioners, however, initially believed that the old Yellowstone Trail route was the better road even though it was three miles longer and included the 10 percent grade of Harrison Hill. It also included a pass that was blocked by snow in the winter and slippery during the spring thaw and following rainstorms. Some highway department engineers claimed that by keeping the highway where it was, it would avoid conflicts with the Northern Pacific Railway, and the old route would be $120,000 cheaper to reconstruct.

While the highway commission opted to keep the route on the original alignment, that decision was not a popular one with area businessmen and tourism promoters. By the first week of June 1927, the commissioners received the first of many telegrams protesting their decision. The Missoula Chamber of Commerce and the Joint County Affairs Committee of Gallatin County both protested the Yellowstone Trail routing of the highway and "urged further consideration of the route thru the Jefferson Canyon." The telegrams were followed up the next day at the commission's monthly meeting by delegations from Whitehall, Bozeman and Three Forks. The delegates all argued that the proposed route through the canyon would "make Lewis and Clark Cavern directly accessible to persons traveling on the main highway and will be more free of snow in the winter time." The highway commissioners stuck to their original argument and hiked the construction costs of the new road up to $150,000. In a concession to the protestors, though, the commission promised to survey both routes before it made a final decision.

In July 1927, a group of citizens from Bozeman, Three Forks, Whitehall, Butte, Deer Lodge and Helena formed the Morrison Cave Development Association (MCDA) to open Lewis and Clark Cavern to the public and promote the construction of a new highway through the Jefferson River canyon. One letter from the organization to Governor John Erickson has survived. In it, the MCDA stated that "an automobile highway to the Cave is absolutely vital."

*A highway will be built down to the Cave sooner or later. The State Highway Commission now has before it two alternative routes in bettering the arterial highway known and the Yellowstone Trail. One of them is the Jefferson Canyon road by Morrison Cave. The other is the circuitous road of Antelope Creek…involving four dangerous railroad crossings, several miles longer, through interminable hills, blocked by snow in winter and condemned by all familiar with local conditions. The citizens working for the opening of the Morrison Cave and the Commercial Clubs of this part of Montana are unanimous in condemning the Antelope Creek routes and in demanding the Jefferson Canyon route.*

MCDA secretary James Gnose of Anaconda threatened "bitter animosities" if the highway commission didn't choose the canyon route. He even went as far as to invoke disgraced highway commissioner Frank Conley's support of the canyon route.

While delegations from Gallatin and Jefferson Counties supported the canyon route, the Madison County commissioners and, especially, State Senator Monte Duncan were vehemently opposed to a road through the Jefferson Canyon. They threw their support behind the existing route via Antelope Creek because it traversed their county and served more people than the proposed canyon route. Duncan continued the fight against the canyon route long after construction was underway in the canyon. He protested the new alignment in the state legislature, claiming that it passed "through a place called Morrison Cave [now Lewis and Clark Cavern], which is inhabited by rattlesnakes, bats, and owls." In early March 1929, Duncan sought to deny the use of gasoline tax money on the canyon route and loudly argued his case to his fellow legislators, newspaper reporters and anybody else who would listen.

The battle between the road supporters and those against it, led by Senator Duncan, heated up in the legislature. In late February 1929, a group of Republican representatives headed by Elmer Johnson of Glasgow introduced House Bill 150, which provided for the amendment of a law passed by the 1927 state legislature. It stipulated how the state would distribute the money collected by the gasoline tax. Duncan, with the support of the Senate Committee on Highways, managed to tag an amendment onto the bill that prevented the spending of gasoline tax money on the Jefferson Canyon road, which was then under construction. A fiery speaker who loudly opposed the highway in no uncertain terms, Duncan enlisted the support of enough of his fellow legislators to also jeopardize the passage of House Bill 94, which would raise the state's existing three-cent gasoline tax to five cents per gallon.

At the time of this political wrangling, the Montana Highway Department was in dire financial straits. In January 1929, state auditors discovered a discrepancy in the amount of gasoline tax refunds due to the counties. When the problem was corrected, the highway commission discovered that there was virtually no money left in the State Highway Fund to match federal money for road construction or for the continued operation of the highway department. The highway commission cut the department's operations to the bare bones, laying off most of its employees and significantly reducing the department's construction program and maintenance operations. Duncan's activities had the potential to further cripple the commission's activities.

Fortunately, cooler heads prevailed in the controversy. Montana's newspapers were generally pro–Good Roads and opposed to Duncan's proposed legislation and his antics at the legislature. Well-built roads clearly benefited the state, while Duncan's grudge against the highway could be catastrophic to the improvement of the state's federal aid highway system. Editorials in the *Helena Independent, Kalispell Daily Inter Lake* and Butte *Montana Standard* chided Duncan for his continued support of the old Yellowstone Trail route. The federal Bureau of Public Roads also made it clear that the passage of HB 150 would have dire consequences for the highway commission's programs and would, essentially, further eviscerate the highway department. Undeterred, Duncan, in a clever parliamentary maneuver, managed to get the hearing for HB 150 placed ahead of HB 94 for the gasoline tax and made HB 94 dependent on HB 150. He also made it clear to his fellow legislators that if HB 150 failed, he would oppose HB 94. While the Senate seemed to support Duncan's amendment at first, the House clearly did not. The House defeated HB 150 in a 43–13 vote, and the five-cent fuel tax law overwhelmingly passed. Although beaten, Duncan vowed to continue the fight against the Jefferson Canyon road—even after the road was completed and open for traffic.

The highway commissioners decided on the route to build by February 1928, when they approved Federal Aid Project No. 248 between Cardwell and Sappington. But it wasn't until July 19, 1928, that the state highway commission awarded a contract to the Leo T. Lawler Company of Butte for the construction of the road through the canyon. The total price for the project was just under $121,000.

While Madison County senator Monte Duncan remained steadfast in his opposition to the canyon route, even after the trouncing he received in the legislature, public opinion was solidly in favor of the new road. A February 1928 editorial in the Butte *Montana Standard* stated:

> *Discussion of this highway project engendered some acrimonious states and brought no little unjust criticism to the hard-working, conscientious members of the state* [highway] *commission. Some people demanded an immediate decision in line with their wishes even before accurate estimates of engineering difficulties and costs could be worked out. The experience should be a lesson to us all in the virtues of harmony, co-operation and consideration for each other. If we are to build up Montana we never can accomplish it by dissension, quibbling, fault-finding and destructive criticism....It is a matter of satisfaction to many that under the highway route selected, Lewis and Clark Cavern, a government monument and a wonderful spectacle, will have the summer parade of tourists passing close by. The route and the substantial obstacles within the canyon certainly guaranteed a "wonderful spectacle" just in the construction of the road for the next two years.*

The Lawler Company had a difficult task ahead of it: the removal of thousands of cubic feet of rock in the canyon to make way for the highway within its five-mile segment. The company began construction on the project shortly after winning the contract in July 1928 and had completed most of the clearing for the proposed route by September. The contractor had graded in a two-mile road westward from the junction of U.S. Highway 287. The company also had a steam shovel with several dump trucks "working down the cliff two miles east of Cardwell." By early October, the seventy-five-man crew was aided by the addition of a gasoline-powered shovel. The contractor anticipated that, as long as the weather held, most of the work on the new route would be completed—with the exception of the heavy rock work in the vicinity of the Lime Spur railroad siding.

The weather certainly didn't cooperate with Lawler's efforts to complete his segment of the road by the highway commission deadline. The company rushed the excavation of rock close to the railroad tracks and continued grading the road. In late November 1928, the blasting of a cliff dropped three hundred tons of rock onto the railroad tracks, forcing the Northern Pacific to temporarily use the Milwaukee Road line on the south bank of the Jefferson River. The work, the *Montana Standard* happily reported, denoted "activity on the part of the contractor in preparation for grading operations next summer." Winter did eventually impose itself on the project, slowing progress but not completely shutting it down. While debate raged in the Montana legislature during the 1929 session about the road, Lawler began drilling for what would be the biggest shot of his time on the road. The company scheduled the dynamiting of 1,600 feet of the 100-foot cliff for April 1929. In what was shaped up to be a media event, the *Montana Standard* claimed that the blast would "attract a swarm of news reel cameramen." Debris from this particular blast would be placed in the river and the railroad tracks moved on top of it to make room for the highway. The blast successfully occurred in late April. Lawler completed his five-mile segment of the new highway by the 1929 deadline imposed on the company by the state highway commission.

On April 26, 1929, the highway commission awarded the next phase of the project to Max Kuney and James Crick of Spokane to build eight miles of highway from milepost 4 to 12. The partners won the contract with their low bid of $107,962. Work began on the segment in May and continued into December 1929. This section also required carving a road between the railroad tracks and the canyon walls but mostly involved building a road across the relatively flat landscape east of the intersection of the road to Lewis and Clark Cavern. Crick and Kuney's work crew had arrived in the area by the end of May 1929 and was quartered at the construction camp at Lime Spur. The clearing and grubbing of the proposed highway alignment began in May, and construction of the road began in earnest in mid-June 1929.

Unlike the five miles built by Lawler, Crick and Kuney's activities did not garner as much media attention. Occasionally, reports appeared in the Butte *Montana Standard* and the *Helena Independent*, usually just noting that work on the highway was "progressing rapidly." As completion of the section and the opening of the entire thirteen-mile length of the new highway neared, however, more articles appeared in local newspapers. Initially, Butte district engineer Homer Smith stated that the road would be opened by mid-November 1929, but unforeseen delays pushed back the official opening until mid-December. Regardless, a *Helena Independent* reporter called the new highway "a scenic road of unusual attraction." It would, the reporter claimed, snip fourteen miles off the old distance between Three Forks and Whitehall and "eliminate entirely the long route up to Harrison and back down the river which, it is said, has been the [cause] of more complaint than any road stretch along [U.S. Highway 10] through Montana."

In early November 1929, the *Montana Standard* interviewed Homer Smith at his office in the Owlsley Block on Park Street in Butte about the new highway. Unfortunately, the interview also involved lingering resentment against state senator Monte Duncan. Smith, who was in a particularly good mood that day, gladly answered all the reporter's questions about the project. Smith said that the Jefferson Canyon segment, the largest project then under construction on U.S. 10, would "have the effect, as soon as it is opened to traffic, of drawing Montana cities located on [U.S. 10] closer together, spiritually and physically, as a result of the activities of the State Highway Commission." It was not, he stated, a particularly difficult road to build, but it did "represent a lot of hard work." The newspaper reporter asked Smith how the grade of the new highway compared to the old Yellowstone Trail alignment.

> [The] *engineer carefully placed himself out of earshot of a picture of Senator "Monte" Duncan of Madison* [County], *who blocked the building of the Jefferson Canyon road for a time in the legislature last winter in the interest of the present route over Harrison hill and said cautiously "Very much better."*

Smith was clearly proud of the new highway and eagerly awaited the completion of the last segment.

Of course, Senator Duncan didn't miss an opportunity to respond to the newspaper article and Smith's comments in particular. In a newspaper editorial that appeared a few days later in the *Montana Standard*, Duncan reiterated his support for the old route. He once again stated his opposition to the Jefferson Canyon route, referring to the "naturally putrid waters of the Jefferson river" and the suckers "wallowing therein" and the bats, rattlesnakes and owls that lived in the cavern. He said that the photos accompanying the November 3 *Montana Standard* article gave people a false sense of the scenic qualities of the canyon, comparing it to views of the Arctic and Antarctic regions—it looks good in photographs, but the actual experience of being there was far different. The editorial was part tongue-in-cheek and part attack on those who supported the canyon route. It was all to no avail, however, as the road officially opened to traffic on December 9, 1929. The old Yellowstone Trail route was relegated to county road status but later designated Secondary Highway 359 in 1945.

The completion of the new highway through Jefferson Canyon created new opportunities for entrepreneurs in the area to tap into the tourist trade. Foremost among these men was Dan LaHood. Born in Lebanon in 1878, he immigrated to the United States in 1899. After arriving in the Whitehall area in 1902, he solicited sales orders for businesses in southwestern Montana until 1909, when he and his wife, Fannie, opened a grocery store at Jefferson Island, a small community on the busy Yellowstone Trail south of Cardwell.

Dan LaHood's Mountain View Hotel was his pride and joy and a popular stopping place for tourists enjoying the local attractions. *Author's collection.*

The underside of the canopy sheltering the gas pumps was illustrated by paintings of area attractions, business advertisements and a map of U.S. 10. *MDT.*

Even before the state highway commission had made its decision on which route U.S. 10 would follow, LaHood had purchased land at the head of head of the Jefferson River Canyon. In the spring of 1928, he began construction of the imposing two-and-a-half-story Mountain View Inn on his property. A carpenter by trade, LaHood built the hotel, gasoline pump canopy and outbuildings himself and completed them in time to host a banquet for the Yellowstone Trail Association shortly after the completion of the road in 1929. By 1935, he had completed construction of several tourist cabins, called the Lewis and Clark Motel, across the new highway from the hotel and christened the new community on Highway 10 "LaHood Park."

In about 1935, Dan LaHood hired Whitehall sign painter Frank Bliss to create signs that were placed on the underside of the canopy protecting the gasoline pumps in front of the hotel. The signs, all wonderful examples of folk art, advertised local sights and businesses and expressed LaHood's support of President Roosevelt's New Deal. A strip map of U.S. Highway 10 (still called the Yellowstone Trail by LaHood) encircled the base of the canopy.

LaHood Park did a thriving business on the highway well into the 1950s, catering primarily to tourist traffic. In 1950, LaHood constructed a separate restaurant adjacent to the hotel on the site of the CCC camp. He also converted the tourist cabins across the road into a more modern motel facility and called it the Lewis and Clark Lodge Motel. Ironically, the construction of Interstate 90 in 1966 bypassed LaHood's operation. Before then, however, Dan LaHood, the "Syrian Volcano," died in Butte in 1957. He was eulogized at his funeral as "little in stature but in an age when big railroad jobs, big mining ventures, and big men were the order of the day, Dan LaHood stood his ground."

The hotel closed shortly after LaHood's death and opened only occasionally as new owners attempted to revitalize the roadside business. For the most part, those endeavors failed, but the restaurant remained a popular stopping place for motorists. The hotel remained little changed from its appearance in 1937 until a fire in 2001 destroyed the building.

The Jefferson River Canyon highway represented a milestone in the highway department's history. A modern paved highway, it highlighted the canyon's spectacular scenery, shortened the distance between Three Forks and Whitehall and provided direct access to Lewis and Clark Cavern. Interstate 90 bypassed the canyon in 1966. But motorists still travel the old road to reach the caverns and continue on through LaHood Park. In every sense, the route is a highway through history.

Chapter 16

# A MONUMENT ABOVE THE WATER

## THE CYR BRIDGE

*T*he Great Depression was a time of big highway and bridge projects. During that tumultuous decade, the Montana Highway Department built over five thousand miles of roadways and constructed nearly two thousand bridges. Most of the bridges were small timber and steel stringer structures, but there were a few enormous bridges as well, like the Missouri River at Culbertson in 1934 and a bridge across the Yellowstone at Billings in 1935.

But the highway department wasn't the only one building roads and bridges in Montana at that time. The federal Bureau of Public Roads (BPR) not only oversaw the state highway commission's programs but also built roads and bridges on National Forest and other federal lands. From 1930 to 1941, the BPR built highways mostly in western and south-central Montana; many BPR bridges still stand. The BPR obtained its funding from Montana's biennial federal aid appropriation. Once a year, representatives from the agency met with the highway commission to determine which federal lands projects would be funded and the money allocated for those projects. The BPR designed and built its own projects with no input from the state. The roads and bridges all met the federal and state design standards, but in the case of bridges, the BPR bridges looked a little different, which makes them easy to distinguish from state-designed bridges.

One of the most spectacular historic bridges in Montana was designed and built by the BPR during the 1930s. The Cyr Bridge crosses the Clark Fork about five miles west of the community of Alberton in Mineral County.

The Bureau of Public Roads intended the Cyr Bridge, a deck truss, to enhance the spectacular scenery of the Alberton Gorge. *Kristi Hager photo, MDT.*

The structure is a five-span, 518-foot steel deck truss bridge, a type becoming increasingly rare in Montana. Located at the head of the Alberton Gorge, which provides a dramatic backdrop for the structure, the Cyr Bridge features nearly three hundred tons of steel in the trusses, spans the river 88 feet above the water and sports the distinctive reinforced concrete guardrails common to BPR bridges.

On August 26, 1932, the BPR awarded a project to Kalispell-based contractor Archie Douglas to build a new six-mile segment of U.S. Highway 10 between Alberton and Cyr on the south and west side of the Clark Fork. A week later, on September 2, the agency signed a $61,853 contract with Nolan Brothers of Minneapolis to build a bridge across the river on the new stretch of roadway. Nolan Brothers had a long history of building road and bridge projects in Montana during the 1920s under the auspices of the state highway commission. The new highway segment and bridge created a shorter and better alignment of U.S. 10. Prior to 1933, the old Yellowstone Trail highway crossed the Clark Fork on the Natural Pier Bridge a mile west of Alberton and then utilized a narrow and treacherous road just a few feet above the river at the base of the Northern Pacific Railway grade. The route crossed the river at the Scenic Bridge four miles west of Cyr.

The contractor began work on the bridge's foundations shortly after winning the contract. Nolan Brothers had to follow the federal government's newly enacted employment regulations, designed to ease the effects of the Great Depression. The contractor ran three five-hour shifts per day, six days a week. Nolan Brothers hired workers entirely from Mineral and Missoula Counties and paid them in cash each week. During the winter of 1933, Nolan Brothers' thirty-five workers erected the falsework and began placement of the steel on the bridge. The contractor hoped to have the steel trusses installed and the falsework removed by the time high water on the Clark Fork made the work difficult in the late spring of 1933. While Nolan Brothers completed the bridge during the first week of July 1933, Archie Douglas, the road contractor, wouldn't complete the approaches to the structure until mid-August 1933. Until then, motorists navigated the old road on the south

The Cyr Bridge is one of the last big deck truss bridges remaining on Montana's highways. *Kristi Hager photo, MDT.*

side of the Clark Fork River. The final cost of the Cyr Bridge was a little less than $64,000. The bridge was an important component of U.S. Highway 10 until it was bypassed by Interstate 90 in 1967.

John Mullan's Big Side Cut section of his wagon road provides the backdrop of the Cyr Bridge. It is one of only a few monumental deck truss bridges remaining in Montana. And like many of the deck trusses no longer existing, it, too, enhances the magnificent scenery of the Treasure State and provides an unforgettable motoring experience for Montanans and tourists. Today, the Cyr Bridge can be best appreciated by the hundreds of kayakers, rafters and fishermen who put in the Clark Fork before the stunning trusses of this unique structure.

Chapter 17

# WHEN GIANT GRASSHOPPERS RULED EASTERN MONTANA

𝓕or tourists and residents alike, picture postcards paint Montana as a wonderland of breathtaking scenery, colorful history, down-to-earth people and weird and wonderful animals—like gargantuan furred trout, jackalopes, house-size cattle and giant grasshoppers. Novelty postcards have been a staple of the Montana tourist trade for over a century. They provide a fun-loving glimpse into the state that not only reflects the myths of the Old West but also shows that its people don't take themselves too seriously and manage to retain their sense of humor in sometimes adverse conditions. The photograph of the smiling young hunter holding a rifle in one hand and an outsized grasshopper by the back legs in the other has been one of the state's most famous novelty postcards for decades. It is second, perhaps, only to the cowboy herding cattle while mounted on the back of an enormous jackrabbit. The hunter with the grasshopper photograph, like many legends, has a basis in fact, one that represents a dark time in Montana's otherwise lively history.

Beginning in the early 1930s, grasshopper swarms that originated in the Dakotas rode wind currents into eastern Montana, where they descended onto the drought-stricken farm fields, devouring everything in their path. Often-heard clichés about how they turned the day into night were not so far-fetched to those unfortunate enough to have experienced them. Oklahoma had its dust bowl and Montana had its grasshoppers during the "Dirty Thirties." Indeed, the grasshopper plague may have made many people sympathetic to the ancient Egyptians who suffered the same fate at the hand of God in the book of Exodus.

Grasshoppers plagued eastern Montana during the Great Depression. Glasgow photographer Cleo Coles lightened the mood with novelty postcards. *MHS Photograph Archives, PAc 2013-50 EXAG.001.*

One of the first mentions of grasshopper plagues in Montana occurred in 1875, when a swarm appeared from the direction of the Sleeping Giant (then called the Bear's Tooth) in the Big Belt Mountains and descended on the Helena Valley. Other blights occurred in the 1880s and 1890s. Since then, grasshopper swarms have struck Montana in regular cycles dependent on climate conditions. A particularly bad infestation occurred in eastern Montana during the 1920s. In an attempt to control them, homesteaders brought in thousands of turkeys to eat the bugs. The birds took care of the insects and made cheap turkey dinners at local diners in eastern Montana a mainstay.

Plagues of grasshoppers seem to coincide with drought and depression. Infestations were an annual occurrence in the state during the Great Depression. The worst one began in July 1938. Within a few weeks of July Fourth, the hoppers had descended on eighteen eastern Montana counties, causing an estimated $6 million in damage to an area that had already seen its share of hardship. A Northwest Airlines pilot encountered a swarm east of Billings at an altitude of seven thousand feet; the swarm was three miles across. There seemed to be no defense against it. Fortunately, the infestation had abated by the end of the summer. Its memory, however, would continue through the efforts of a Montana photographer with an eye for the quirky.

Some people are lucky enough to see humor and opportunity in adversity. There wasn't much of either in eastern Montana during the 1930s, but a Glasgow photographer bucked the trend and created a masterpiece. In 1937 or 1938, Glasgow photographer Cleo Coles asked one of his neighbors to pose for his most famous photograph. John "Bud" Nass was the nineteen-year-old son of Joseph and Theresa Nass, who operated a tourist cabin camp and men's clothing store in Glasgow. Bud had recently graduated from high school and was employed at his father's Federated Clothing Store in Glasgow.

In 1938, Coles began selling copies of the photograph, under the titles "Grasshopper Shot Near Fort Peck Dam" and "Giant Grasshopper Shot Near Vernholt's Drugstore at Fort Peck Dam," along with several other novelty postcards he had produced. These include one of a giant grasshopper riding a burro, another of a cowboy roping a giant grasshopper and a postcard showing a grasshopper towing an insecticide spreader. The postcards sold briskly from Coles's photography studio and at outlets all over northeastern Montana. His most famous postcard, "Grasshopper Shot Near Fort Peck Dam," sold well over 100,000 copies by the time he stopped keeping count.

Born in Missouri in 1908, Cleo Coles developed an interest in photography while growing up on a dairy farm in Minnesota. He and a friend came west to Montana in 1934 to photo-document the construction of the massive Fort Peck Dam. By all accounts, Coles was an excellent photographer, selling photos to *Life* magazine and the *Saturday Evening Post*. Some of his most famous photos were of the Fort Peck slide that took the lives of eight men in September 1938 and of Franklin Roosevelt's visit to the construction site in 1937.

Another famous postcard Coles produced during that period shows two thermometers side by side, one side reading 110 degrees in July and the other 65 degrees below zero in January; it was second in popularity to the giant grasshopper postcard. Coles eventually opened a studio in Glasgow and continued to document the construction of the dam. In 1946, he relocated his studio to Malta, moving back to Glasgow in 1962. He died there in April 1970. During his long and successful career, Coles specialized in portrait photos and was the first photographer in Montana to both shoot and process his own color photographs.

Bud Nass, the young man who bagged the giant grasshopper, also had a long and successful career in Montana. Aside from being immortalized on the postcard, he served as a gunner in the U.S. Army Air Force in World War II, was a dry goods store owner in northeastern Montana and was a member of the Montana State Highway Commission from 1963 to 1971. At the time of his death in 1976, Nass was owner of the Federated Store he worked at as a youth when the famous postcard was made and vice president of the Glasgow Chamber of Commerce. Later accounts of his life always mentioned him as the man who posed for the picture with the giant grasshopper.

Novelty postcards, like the giant grasshopper series, fit perfectly with the way Montanans were trying to pass off the state, not only as the quintessential embodiment of the Old West, but also as a place of magnificent scenery, colorful western characters, enormous semi-sized sugar beets, jackalopes, furred trout and giant insects. They certainly make things a lot bigger in Montana, and tourists ate it up, creating an industry that still thrives today.

# Chapter 18

# MONTANA'S HIGHWAY MUSE

## BOB FLETCHER AND THE ROADSIDE HISTORICAL MARKERS

*F*or many Montanans and tourists, their knowledge of Montana's colorful past is based on what they've read on roadside historical markers. For nearly a century, they have been an important part of Montana's transportation landscape and, along with the highway maps, are all that remains of the state's Golden Age of Automobile Tourism of the 1930s. But like many things, the markers have changed over time as interpretation of important historical events has changed and audiences have become more sophisticated. Today, there are nearly three hundred roadside historical and geological markers gracing the state's highways and rest areas. The story of the historical markers is an important one and one that is the brainchild of a remarkable man, Robert H. "Bob" Fletcher.

Montana owes much to Bob Fletcher. He was a true renaissance man with myriad interests and talents. A native of Wisconsin, he came to Montana in the early twentieth century with the U.S. Reclamation Service, fell in love with the place and never left. Although a civil engineer by training, he became a troubadour for the American West, a raconteur of colorful stories about the Montana frontier and a master of the art of Old West dialect. He was a cowboy poet (before they were called that) and an expert in the golden age of the Montana cattle industry. Importantly, he was the father of the modern Montana tourism industry and the writer of one of the anthems of the American West, "Don't Fence Me In."

Fletcher went to work for the highway department after Montana voters passed a substantial gasoline tax law in 1927. The Good Roads Law put the department in the driver's seat for road design and construction. Fletcher's initial job at the department was to review highway plans and act, at times, as an intermediary between the engineers and the contractors. It was a job the gregarious Fletcher was particularly good at. The Great Depression hit Montana in full force starting in 1930. As county tax bases dwindled, gas tax revenues dropped precipitously, largely stopping any new construction until 1931. That year, the state legislature passed a $5 million debenture to provide matching money for federal funds. It also coincided with the Hoover administration providing emergency funding to the states for road projects. Montana benefited from the program and Franklin Roosevelt's New Deal beginning in 1933.

Bob Fletcher developed much of Montana's first automobile tourism program during the height of the Great Depression. *MHS Photograph Archives, Helena, 942-134.*

Highway and bridge construction boomed with the New Deal. Over the course of the next eight years, the highway department increased its staff and managed to improve nearly five thousand miles of primary, secondary and urban roads and build over fifteen hundred bridges. Modern paved roads would, the state highway commission hoped, draw people to the state who would stay awhile, enjoy the scenery and the recreational opportunities Montana had to offer and, importantly, spend money. Highway improvements, better automobiles and an improving economy jump-started what would become the Golden Age of Automobile tourism in Montana.

The Montana Highway Department, as the keeper of the state's highways, became the principal outfit in the development of Montana's first true automobile tourism program. In 1934, the commission put Bob Fletcher in charge of developing the program. His first product was a highway map designed specifically for tourists. They were easy to read and colorful and fit nicely in an automobile's glove compartment. All were illustrated by the commission's graphic artist, Irvin "Shorty" Shope. Next came stone monuments at the entry points to the state. The port of entry program began in 1935 and welcomed tourists to Montana (see chapter 19). Fletcher wrote, and Shope and Dan Gough illustrated, brochures and pamphlets that were distributed across the country.

In May 1935, Fletcher proposed to the highway commission a plan to write, fabricate and install historical markers along the state's highways. The commissioners liked the idea and gave him $5,000 to do it. Fletcher had already written the texts for most of them. All were done in a folksy style that related, essentially, a Hollywood version of Montana history—in two hundred words or fewer. He wanted tourists to feel like a cowboy was leaning up against their car, rolling a cigarette and telling them a story in a way only a cowboy could do it. The highway department's sign painter, Ace Kindrick, hand painted the lettering on plywood boards. Highway department maintenance men mounted the signs on log posts embedded in native rock bases. Shope designed and embellished the decorative crosspieces from which the signs hung.

By the end of 1935, highway department maintenance men had installed 28 markers along the highways. Three years later, 98 markers stood along the highways and 114 in 1941, the year Fletcher resigned from the highway department. The markers were a hit with Montanans and tourists right from the beginning. The *New Yorker* magazine raved, "In Montana the signs are worth reading....So far as I know, these are the only official road signs in any state of America which dare to be light-hearted or colloquial." Montana newspaper editors loved them:

> [The] *second experiment this year is the historical markers, written by Bob Fletcher of the Highway department, who combines a gift for concise phrasing with a swell sense of humor....There are a lot of good stories, and they're enormously effective on hardwood, decorated with western drawings, placed where they happened. You have the background, looking untouched since then, you see the pictures under Fletcher's phrasings.*

Ernie Pyle, the renowned war correspondent, crowed, "Montana makes its history a thing of joy instead of a stodgy sermon."

There were some problems though. The marker texts were hand-lettered on the sign boards, and misspellings were chronic to them. Whether Fletcher was the bad speller or Kindrick is not known. Sometimes the grammar was bad. Another was in the phrasing. The Wolf Point marker talked about the origins of the city as a steamboat port and the fact that hunters brought wolf hides there for shipment downriver on steamboats. The hides would be stacked along the riverbank in the winter, and when the spring came, they thawed. Fletcher stated in the original text for the marker, "Even a blind man with a cane could find the place." People of

From 1935 to 1941, the Montana Highway Department installed 114 roadside historical markers. All featured hand-lettered sign boards and rock bases. *MDT.*

Wolf Point and the Assiniboine tribe took issue with the wording, and the sentence was removed.

The Blackfeet chopped the Blackfeet Nation sign into kindling, allegedly because it was Frank Bird Linderman's information about the tribe that went on the board. They apparently didn't like Linderman. One quote didn't go over well with the sign's female readers, "They didn't care how much the tribes fought amongst themselves. They were like the old timer whose wife was battling a grizzly bear. He said he never had seen a fight where he took so little interest in the outcome."

The historical markers were, essentially, a Hollywood version of Montana's history—simple, easy to understand, colorful and told in a way that evoked the Old West. Fletcher didn't always let the facts get in the way of a good story, and he used descriptions of Native Americans that were acceptable at the time but are not today. Most were definitely fun to read:

> *Take it by and large, the old West produced some tolerably lurid gun toters. Their hole card was a single-action frontier model .45 Colt and their long*

*suit was fanning it a split second quicker than similarly inclined gents. This talent sometimes postponed their obsequies a while, providing they weren't pushed into taking up rope spinning from the loop end of a lariat by a wearied public. Through choice or force of circumstances these people sometimes threw in with the "Wild Bunch";—rough-riding, fast-shooting hombres, prone to disregard the customary respect accorded other people's brands. (Early Day Outlaws)*

and

*Time was when ox and mule teams used to freight along this route. A 5-ton truck doesn't look as picturesque but there hasn't been much change in the language of the drivers. Jerk line skinners were plumb fluent when addressing their teams. They got right earnest and personal. It was spontaneous—no effort about it. When they got strung out they were worth going a long ways to hear. As a matter of fact you didn't have to go a long ways, providing your hearing was normal. Adjectives came natural to them but they did bog down on some names. They had the same name for each of their string. Those times are gone forever. The day of the ox has given way to the era of bull. (Freighters)*

Even though Fletcher left the department in 1941 to work for the Montana Power Company, he continued to write marker texts, under contract, for a few years after World War II ended.

Bob Fletcher retired from the Montana Power Company in 1964 but remained active in the state. He served for many years on the board of directors of the Montana Historical Society and wrote articles for the society's journal, *Montana: The Magazine of Western History*. In 1960, he wrote *Free Grass to Fences: The Montana Cattle Range Story* for the historical society. It remains one of the definitive histories of the Montana cattle industry. Bob Fletcher died in November 1972. But his legacy lives on in the highway maps and in the roadside historical marker program. For many, Fletcher's version of the state's colorful history is the one best remembered by Montanans and visitors alike.

Chapter 19

# WELCOME TO MONTANA!

## THE PORTS OF ENTRY STATIONS

*T*he Lima rest area on Interstate 15 in southwestern Montana includes a relic from the Montana Department of Transportation's past: a vintage port of entry station. The building functions much as it originally did, providing a place for motorists to stop, stretch their legs and get their first taste of Montana's scenic beauty. Old port of entry stations, once a common sight on Montana's highways, are rare. Another is located on the grounds of the department's Missoula District office on West Broadway in Missoula. It functions as the local highway maintenance office.

The 1930s was a time of incredible change for the state's highways, as the Montana Highway Department spent millions of federal dollars to upgrade roads and bridges. During a span of just over ten years, the state's highways transformed from among the nation's worst to one of the country's best road systems. A benefit of that change was a huge surge in the number of tourists visiting the state. The highway department responded by initiating a national ad campaign, distributing free highway maps and promotional brochures, building roadside picnic areas and installing roadside historical markers. An important part of the program was the establishment of port of entry stations at nine locations near the state's borders. The stations were on the front line of Montana's tourist industry for three decades.

The stations originated in 1935 as shacks where traffic industry survey checkers operated in conjunction with State Department of Agriculture inspectors. Their initial purpose was simply to count the number of out-of-state vehicles entering the state. It is not known what caused the

Tourists stopping at the stations for information received a sticker on their windshields identifying them as Montana guests. *Author's collection.*

transformation of the survey into the information posts they became the following year. The stations were open from mid-June until mid-September each summer in conjunction with college summer vacation. Attendants at the stations were all college students who "talk well, look well, know their state and have manners." The department assigned two attendants to each station. The Missoula port of entry station had three attendants. Signs at the state's borders asked out-of-state tourists to stop at the stations. If they did, the attendants, who sported uniforms similar to gas station employees, provided each car with maps and other promotional materials, answered questions and slapped a "Guest" sticker, decorated with a photograph of a Native American man in full regalia, on the windshield.

From 1936 to 1951, port of entry station attendants wore distinctive uniforms, but in 1952, the department changed the outfit to include blue jeans, a western-style shirt, a bolo tie and a straw cowboy hat. The highway commissioners hired attendants after a rigorous selection process. Occasionally, even the governor participated in hiring station attendants. By the late 1950s, the highway commissioners debated the continued need for the port of entry stations (renamed tourist courtesy stations in 1954), especially after the Federal Aid Highway Act of 1956 launched the interstate highway program. An inventory of the thirteen stations conducted by the highway department in 1957 showed that most were run-down and in dire need of upgrades. The description of the station at Rockvale, at the intersection of U.S. Highways 212 and 310, described it as needing "running water, toilets, refrigerator, modern stove. Cesspool next door drains onto open ground 30 feet behind the station and gives tourists a greeting of its own." The West Yellowstone station was located at a "favorite turn around point for off-duty park employees and confused travelers. It also is too accessible to [town] and attendants assigned there spend too many duty hours in town." The impending interstate program and needed renovations proved enough for the highway commission to permanently shut down the stations after the 1957 season. Instead, the commission ordered that the department's Planning Survey Division just maintain traffic counts of tourist traffic.

During the 1950s, the port of entry station near Columbia Falls saw traffic entering and leaving Glacier National Park. *MHS Photograph Archives, Helena, PAc 76-82.6-D-402.*

The Lima Port of Entry station was originally located fifteen miles to the south on U.S. Highway 91 at Monida. The rustic building was constructed in 1936 from standardized plans developed by the Montana Highway Department and intended to give the appearance of a log cabin. When built, the station had no electricity or running water, and the closest spring was one and a half miles away. To keep drinks cold, the attendants buried a box in the ground, kept it filled with ice or cool water and tightly sealed it with a lid. The only telephone in the community was at the general store and was only available for use during business hours. The highway department had trouble keeping people at the remote station and decided to move the building to Lima in 1948.

Like all port of entry stations, the building contained two rooms: a foyer and living quarters for the two attendants. The living area included two beds, a counter, cupboards and two closets. The 1957 highway department report provides the best description of the Lima Port of Entry station:

*Old building but the station has been well kept. Needs toilets—attendants receive frequent requests for restrooms here. Needs running water—it now has a good fountain outside the building, which is popular with visitors. Needs modern stove, one to provide some warmth on cold mornings as well as to be used for cooking. Needs shades on the west windows.*

The description of the station indicates that it was in much better shape than most of the older stations in Montana by then.

The Lima station was one of the busiest in the state. The pressure must have been too much for one attendant in 1956, because he quit about midway through the summer, leaving one man, D.C. Hodges, to man the station by himself for two months. The highway commissioners commended Hodges for his dedication to the job, doubled his salary during those two months and gave him a $150 bonus.

After the station closed in 1957, it functioned as storage at the MDT's Lima maintenance shop for the next fifty years. Amazingly, both the exterior and interior of the building were not changed, except for the addition of a sink in the interior. Intact port of entry stations are rare in Montana, and the Lima station is an excellent representation of what was once an important part of the state's tourism industry. It has been moved onto a concrete foundation at the new rest area and functions as an interpretive site for the local historical society. So come on down to Lima, check out the new rest area and perhaps somebody calling, "Howdy, stranger, welcome to Montana!" will step out of the old station and, once again, welcome people to the Treasure State.

# Chapter 20

# THE LAUREL ROADSIDE MUSEUM

*D*espite the crippling effects of the Great Depression, America was a country on the move in the 1930s. Thousands of American motorists took to the roads to inspect the country's scenic wonders and take advantage of its recreational opportunities. Montana and the Montana Highway Department were more than willing to accommodate them. The responsibility for promoting tourism in the Treasure State fell to the highway department and its plans engineer, Bob Fletcher. Beginning in 1934 with the first "official" highway map, Fletcher, with the blessing of the State Highway Commission, developed an ambitious program to draw tourists to the state and keep them here as long as possible by promoting its natural resources and colorful history. To that end, Fletcher oversaw the creation of the highway historical markers in 1935, roadside picnic areas, information centers, the ports of entry stations, the acquisition of Pictograph Cave outside Billings and the establishment of a roadside museum program in 1938.

Fletcher planned the roadside museums as joint efforts between the highway department and local chambers of commerce or commercial clubs. He envisioned a chain of fifteen roadside museums across the state, each devoted to a single subject, such as geology, paleontology, wildlife, history, industrial resources and Indian culture. Each museum would include dioramas, specimens, models, photographs and maps. An "alert, well-informed attendant" would manage each museum to provide tourists with information about its displays and other local attractions. Fletcher

*Above*: Roadside museums to exhibit artifacts, paintings and dioramas about Montana history were part of Bob Fletcher's schemes to promote tourism in the state. *MDT.*

*Opposite*: A member of the Crow tribe, Max Big Man curated the Laurel museum in the late 1930s and early 1940s. *MHS Photograph Archives, Helena, Lot 035, B11F04.03.*

contacted chambers of commerce in cities along U.S. Highways 2, 10 and 91, eventually interesting several communities in the plan. The highway department developed the architectural design for the museums and would build them, but it was up to local organizations to staff and maintain them. The rustic buildings were built by Works Progress Administration labor with materials furnished by the highway department.

In March 1938, the *Laurel Outlook* announced that the Montana Highway Department would build a museum in Northern Pacific Park at the junction of U.S. Highways 10 and 310 in Laurel. The design accompanying the article showed a rustic log building with a cobblestone veneered foundation that was similar in design to the highway department's information centers and ports of entry stations. The two-room building would also house the city's police department and an information center. The Laurel Commercial Club hired Max Big Man, an Apsáalooke (Crow) Indian from the Hardin area, to curate the museum and provide lectures on Indian life to tourists. He and his family lived in three tepees set up in the park near the museum. A black bear named Susie lived in a cage on the museum grounds between

203   Chief Max Big Man

two of the tepees. Bob Fletcher built the exhibit cases in the museum and provided most of the artifacts shown in them. Indeed, he acquired the stone tools exhibited at the Laurel museum from Pictograph Cave archaeological site outside Billings. The department's graphic artist, Ervin "Shorty" Shope, created the dioramas, including one depicting the arrival of man in the region. Other exhibits included fossils, dinosaur bones and a large mounted bison head loaned by local businessmen.

Max Big Man was a force to be reckoned with during the 1930s and 1940s. Born on the Crow Reservation in 1889 and a graduate of Haskell Institute, Big Man was already a well-known lecturer and author when hired by the Laurel Commercial Club to manage the museum. He lived on the site with family. His job was to answer questions posed by tourists and generally function as an "entertainer," according to local newspapers. Many of Big Man's artifacts and beadwork were on display in the museum. His prized reed flute was also on display. Occasionally, he would remove it from the display case and play the instrument for the tourists. After his stint at the Laurel roadside museum, Max Big Man went on to operate a souvenir shop near the Little Bighorn Battlefield and serve on the Crow tribal council. He died in 1950.

As envisioned by Fletcher, each museum would have a particular theme. Some would concentrate on local industries, natural resources of the region, local traditions and history. The Laurel museum featured five dioramas that described the region's prehistory; each case contained fossils from different geological eras. During the 1938 tourist season, the museum hosted twelve thousand visitors. Although the highway department erected signs directing motorists to the museum in Northern Pacific Park, many stopped after hearing about the exhibits. An article in the *Billings Gazette* reported that the displays were "the cause of much comment. This [was] especially noticeable among professional people, teachers, and students....We have been told that the word has gone a long way in all directories, for many people say they were advised by others to stop here and examine the dioramas, see the specimens, and hear Max Big Man's lectures."

Bob Fletcher toured the state during the off-seasons in an attempt to interest other communities in building roadside museums. Missoula and Great Falls definitely showed some interest in the scheme, but only Dillon actively sought to establish a museum on U.S. 91. It is unclear, however, if a museum was ever built there. While Fletcher had big plans for the scheme, only one other museum was built.

By all accounts, the Laurel museum was a popular tourist attraction for motorists on their way to and from Yellowstone National Park over the newly opened Beartooth Highway. Laurel Commercial Club member J.F. MacDonald boasted that much of the museum's popularity was based on word of mouth. He estimated that during the summers, up to one hundred people a day visited the museum in Laurel—some, in fact, stopping twice to take in the informative exhibits and listen to Big Man's popular lectures. For four years, the museum opened its doors to visitors every Memorial Day and closed down for the season on the Labor Day weekend.

Pearl Harbor changed everything. The federal government withdrew most of its funding to state highway departments to pay for the war. For the first time since 1933, the Montana Highway Department lost employees as they left to join the military or to take jobs in the war industries on the West Coast. The state's highway program nearly ceased to exist, as funds could only be spent on strategically important highways with the authorization of the War Department. After the Laurel museum closed down in September 1941, it never reopened as a tourist attraction. By 1945, the Laurel Police Department was the sole occupant of the entire building. It is not known what happened to the dioramas, models and artifacts that decorated the museum.

Despite the apparent success of the Laurel museum, the idea did not catch on in the other cities that expressed interest in the program. The Highway Commission built a museum at Pictograph Cave outside Billings in 1938, but vandalism and fire caused it to close down by 1945. When the Billings Commercial Club wanted to open a museum across U.S. Highway 87 from the Yellowstone County Fairgrounds in Billings in 1939, the highway commission offered only the land upon which the museum would be located. The Laurel museum was the crown jewel of the highway department's tourism programs during the Great Depression. Although ultimately a failure, the museum inspired the construction of other roadside attractions by private individuals during the 1950s and 1960s, many of which are still located next to Montana's highways. The Laurel museum still exists and is located in Fireman's Park in Laurel. The building is currently occupied by the Laurel Chamber of Commerce and was recently rehabilitated.

Chapter 21
# THE SMITH MINE AND BEARCREEK

*T*hat Montana's roads were important to its rich history is borne out by the large number of historic sites that can be seen adjacent to them. Motorists may note them, but often they don't know the history behind these sometimes significant, but often ordinary, places. Sometimes, though, a site stands next to the road that draws a lot of attention, but maybe not for the reasons initially believed.

On a lonely stretch of Montana Secondary 308 east of Red Lodge, there is a collection of deteriorated corrugated metal structures standing sentinel across a gulch from the highway. The structures are all that remain of one of the state's most important and tragic industrial sites, the Smith Mine. In 1889, a group of Boston entrepreneurs, headed by Elijah Smith, formed the Montana Coal and Iron Company to mine coal in the Bear Creek mining district. Although it was only one of several coal mines in the district, the Smith Mine boasted the most extensive network of tunnels and an impressive processing plant aboveground for the coal.

Bear Creek coal was the gold standard for high-grade coal mined in Montana. It was well suited for use in the Anaconda smelter, by the Northern Pacific Railway and for homes and businesses across the state. The mines drew hundreds of men and their families to the district. Most were immigrants from eastern and northern Europe. Two communities, Washoe and Bearcreek, grew up near the mines. Both were rough-and-tumble mining camps. By 1920, the district boasted a population of a few thousand people living in the mining camps and in the gulches adjacent to the mines. The Yellowstone Park Railway built a short-line railroad from Bridger to the mines in 1906.

The remains of the Smith Mine stand forlornly next to Secondary 308, providing little indication of the tragic event that happened there in 1943. *MDT.*

In anticipation of the arrival of the railroad, George Lamport and his son-in-law and business partner, Robert Leavens, purchased land a couple miles east of the mines in 1905 and formed the Bearcreek Town and Improvement Company. Lots in the new community of Bearcreek sold quickly as mining expanded in the district. Within a few months of the community's founding, the *Red Lodge Picket* reported, "Bearcreek is showing signs of thrift and activity each succeeding day. At present fourteen stores have been opened up or are about ready to start for business, the buildings yet unfinished receiving the last touches." By December 1906, the town had incorporated, had a post office and had begun construction of concrete sidewalks, a telephone system, a city water system and electric streetlights. The town incorporated in 1906 but never had an official police force, and no church was ever built there. The *Picket* reported in August 1906:

> *The future of the little city of Bearcreek may not be written until some other day. Its location is not the most desirable, topographically speaking,*

*for a city of extensive magnitude. That it is destined to become one of the greatest coal mining camps in the entire western country, is an assured fact, and those who are acquainted with the lay of the country say that further down the valley, a short distance, may be found a location for a fine residence district. At present the town is growing rapidly, no less than ten buildings being in [the] course of construction. Among these are a building that is being erected by B.E. Vaill in which a bank will be established, a business building adjoining it...three other businesses and a number of dwelling houses.*

By end of the year, 250 miners (about half of the population of the district) were working in the four commercial mines operating in the district, including the Montana Coal and Iron Company's Smith Mine two miles west of town. The coal mines attracted immigrants from Serbia, Croatia, Montenegro, Italy and Scotland. As in other mining camps, ethnic groups settled together in neighborhoods in Bearcreek. From 1906 to 1921, Bearcreek suffered from a chronic housing shortage. Despite the lack of good housing, Bearcreek boomed in the first decade of the twentieth century.

By 1910, Bearcreek claimed a population of 302 people. The mines employed about half the adult male population of the community. The commercial district had expanded to include twenty-three businesses, including ten saloons. The Carbon County Chamber of Commerce touted Bearcreek's main street as

*the center of a district that is destined to become famous for its building stone. There is a brickyard there and other industries in the first stages of development. There are two hotels, one as fine as can be found in this part of the country...a bank, lumberyard, furniture store, drug store, jewelry store, two butcher shops, two restaurants, livery and feed stables, barber shops, stage lines and one of the finest water systems in the world, a splendid electrical-light system, besides many small stores, lodging houses and telephone exchanges. The town is the center of a population of about 1,200, which includes the mining communities and the outlook is for an increase in the population within the next year.*

The city's economy, however, was based on the ability of the mines to ship coal out on the Yellowstone Park Railway, renamed the Montana, Wyoming and Southern (MW&S) Railway in 1909. Unfortunately, the

Bearcreek once boasted a population of several hundred people and was a cosmopolitan city in its heyday. *MHS Photograph Archives, Helena, PAc 76-118.M1.*

railroad was dependent on the Northern Pacific Railway, which provided coal cars to the railroad for the shipment of coal out of the mines. The Northern Pacific, therefore, had indirect control of the fortunes of the Bear Creek district and Bearcreek. Even considering its reliance on the seeming vagaries of the railroad, Carbon County was the dominant coal producer in Montana, with Bearcreek providing the necessary services to the miners working one of the richest underground coal mines in the northern Rockies, the Smith Mine.

The coal industry in south-central Montana waned after World War I, initiating a downturn in the Bear Creek mines. The MW&S remained dependent on the Northern Pacific, which often withheld coal cars from the mines. The precarious economic condition was aggravated by the Northern Pacific's increasing reliance on coal strip-mined at Colstrip and by the growing popularity of alternate fuels, such as natural gas, for domestic purposes. Bearcreek's commercial district remained intact during the 1920s, but hard economic times during the 1930s caused a profound change in the city's appearance. In 1935, the Bearcreek High School's newspaper reported, "Such a thing as passing a house on the road is not unusual to anyone around here. At the rate the houses are being moved, we may need a traffic cop to 'let the houses go by!'" Many folks burned down their buildings for the insurance money or because they couldn't afford the property taxes.

Perhaps the best way to experience the old Bearcreek today is in the lonely cemetery on the hillside a mile east of town. In June 1909, Bearcreek founders George and Lodenia Lamport and Robert and Ella Leavens conveyed four acres to the City of Bearcreek for use as a cemetery. Red Lodge city surveyor Fred Hine surveyed and laid out the site of the burial ground. He designed it to include a simple circular pathway traversed by roads entering the cemetery from the north, south, east and west and intersecting in the center of the parcel. The cemetery consisted of 204 burial plots. The first interment in the new cemetery occurred on November 28, 1909, when six-year-old Helen Markovich's parents laid her to rest there.

Today, the Bearcreek Cemetery holds 474 burials occupying about two acres inhabited now mostly by rattlesnakes. The cemetery provides an excellent cross-section of Bearcreek's population during its peak years, with a variety of different headstones representing all the ethnic groups that once lived in the town. Most markers are simple, but a few are more sophisticated. Many eastern European graves are clearly identified by the distinctive Cyrillic lettering and photographs of the dead embedded in porcelain medallions. Sadly, a large number of children are buried there, attesting to the high infant mortality rate in the former coal camp. A stone monument, placed in 1947, commemorates the victims of the Smith Mine disaster. Twenty-two men who died in the mine in February 1943 are buried in the cemetery.

During the Great Depression, the Smith Mine was the largest employer in the district. Coal mining suffered during the Depression but rebounded in 1942 after the United States became embroiled in World War II. By 1943, the mine was operating seven days a week, twenty-four hours a day. Many of the miners worked double shifts or on their usual days off to make as much money as possible before peace ended the boom. The working conditions in the Smith Mine, however, were not the best, and the Montana Coal and Iron Company was far from a responsible employer. It was a dry mine with coal dust thick in the air and a ventilation system totally inadequate to the task of circulating the air. As with many underground coal mines, there were pockets of methane gas to make things even more

On February 27, 1943, a coal dust explosion and carbon monoxide killed seventy-four men at the Smith Mine. *MHS Photograph Archives, Helena, Lot 026 B605.03.*

dangerous. The company, anxious to maximize its profits during the war, failed to provide adequate safety measures. Men working underground still utilized open-flame carbide lamps, and many miners smoked while on shift.

At 9:37 a.m. on February 27, 1943, smoke followed by a hurricane-force wind blew from the entrance to the No. 3 mine, the first indication of trouble underground. "There's something wrong down here. I'm getting out," the hoist operator called up. He and two nearby miners were the last men to leave the mine alive. A pocket of methane apparently ignited underground, causing a coal dust explosion that killed many men instantly. Others were soon overcome by carbon monoxide gas; many survivors barricaded themselves inside tunnels, fruitlessly waiting for rescue.

The families of the seventy-four men trapped underground likely knew that help wouldn't reach them in time. Rescue crews, some from as far away as Butte, Roundup and Cascade County, worked around the clock to clear debris and search for survivors. There were none. Some men died as a result of the explosion, but most fell victim to the deadly carbon monoxide gas released by the blast. The historical marker overlooking the site describes the Smith Mine disaster and the simple message left by two miners trapped underground after the explosion, waiting for the poisonous gas they knew would come.

> *Walter & Johnny. Good-bye.*
> *Wives and daughters. We died*
> *an easy death. Love from us both.*
> *Be good.*

The tragedy sparked investigations at the state and national level that resulted in improvements in mine safety. The exact cause of the explosion has never been determined.

The Smith Mine disaster and the closure of the mine after the abandonment of the MW&S Railroad in 1953 virtually guaranteed that the depressed economy in the Bear Creek District would continue for the foreseeable future. The population of Bearcreek dropped from 237 individuals in 1950 to only 61 in 1960, making it the smallest incorporated city in Montana at that time. In 1963, newspaper reporter Faye Kuhlman and her husband moved to Bearcreek from Billings. Recognizing the potential of the near ghost town as an artists' and retirement community, Kuhlman began publication of small mimeographed histories of the community and actively promoted the sale of city lots that were owned by the county. Through her efforts, the city restored the Bearcreek Bank building and caused a revitalization of the community that has been ongoing for more than forty years. Bearcreek is the second-smallest incorporated city in Montana (Ismay is the smallest) with, perhaps, the cemetery on the lonely hillside east of town the only reminder of its once vibrant history.

Chapter 22

# THE DELL FLIGHT STRIP

*T*he Montana Department of Transportation (MDT) is much more than highways and bridges. An important part of the agency is the Aeronautics Division. The State of Montana created the Montana Aeronautics Commission in 1945. The commission became part of MDT's operations in 1991. It is responsible for the maintenance of state-owned airports, the promotion of safety in aeronautics and administering loans and grants programs to municipal governments for airport development and improvement projects. Sixteen state-owned airports are managed by the Aeronautics Division. One of those, the Dell Flight Strip in the state's southwest corner, has a connection to Montana's contribution to the effort during the Second World War.

The Bureau of Air Commerce built an emergency runway and beacon near Dell in early November 1935. A few months prior, the U.S. Department of Commerce's Bureau of Air Commerce began improvements on the National Parks Airway route between Dell and Helena. The agency established the airway route in 1928 but had only developed it as far as Monida Pass by 1931. The improvement of the route in Montana coincided with the delineation and lighting of the Northern Transcontinental Airway route, also in 1935. Improvements to the National Parks Airway included the installation of ten beacons and the construction of emergency airfields to provide landing areas for aircraft in trouble or because of adverse weather conditions.

In the wake of the U.S. entry into World War II, the U.S. Army established East Base in Great Falls and satellite airfields at Cut Bank, Lewistown and Glasgow in 1942. The purpose of the satellite bases was training B-17 Flying Fortress crews in high-altitude pinpoint bombing techniques that would be used in the European and Pacific theaters of operation. Improvements at the satellite airfields included hangars, barracks, mess and rec halls, Norden bombsight vaults and support structures for the training operations. Also included was the construction of landing fields in outlying areas that bomber crews could use in case of emergency. One of those emergency landing fields for B-17 bombers was just outside the community of Dell in southern Beaverhead County.

In June or early July 1942, "at the instigation of the [U.S.] Army," the federal Public Roads Administration asked the State Highway Commission to obtain the right-of-way necessary for and to construct an emergency flight strip at Dell. The federal government would pay for the project, but the design of the runway and the property itself would be the responsibility of the highway commission. To that end, the Montana Highway Department's Right-of-Way Bureau acquired the land in July 1942 and secured agreements from surrounding landowners in regard to height restrictions for agricultural buildings "that might endanger planes using the strip." In late August 1942, the army announced plans to construct roadside flight strips in Montana; the first one would be built at Dell. From 1942 to 1945, the Montana Highway Department functioned at a minimal level since the federal government directed funds ordinarily targeted for highway construction be used for the war effort. The army intended to build the airstrips adjacent to strategic highways, such as U.S. Highway 91.

On December 17, 1942, the highway commission awarded the project to the Minneapolis-based Barnard-Curtiss Company to build the airfield. The company relied primarily on out-of-state labor for the project, but a fair number of local men, including teenagers, also worked on building the runway. Highway department engineer Sam Thompson supervised construction of the strip. The army and highway commission imposed a deadline of June 30, 1943, to complete the project. Work on the airstrip didn't begin until May 1943, and Barnard-Curtiss finally completed work on the airfield in the first week of October 1943, over two months past the deadline. Using readily available resources from the area, much of the infrastructure at the Civil Aviation Authority's nearby emergency landing field was relocated to the newly constructed flight strip. This included the beacon tower and light, electrical shed, boundary markers and lighted

During World War II, the United States Army Air Force intended the Dell Flight Strip as an emergency landing field for Flying Fortress bombers. *MDT.*

delineators. From 1943 to 1944, the flight strip also served as an emergency landing field for military aircraft ferried to East Base in Great Falls by Women Airforce Service Pilots (WASP). In 1944, the military suspended the B-17 training operations in Montana. While the airstrip did occasionally accommodate emergency landings by private aircraft, it is unknown if the flight strip ever saw an emergency landing by a Flying Fortress. By 1949 and without military support, highway department Right-of-Way Bureau supervisor A.G. Swaney reported that he didn't "believe that very much had been done by way of maintenance on the strip by state forces."

While the Dell Flight Strip was constructed anticipating possible use by the military, its service to the general local community proved much more important after World War II ended in 1945. Evidence suggests that pilots used it primarily for recreational purposes, as it provided easy access to blue ribbon trout streams. It also served as a base for search-and-rescue operations, was used by crop dusters, was the site of aircraft instructional classes and provided a convenient emergency landing strip. In the later twentieth and early twenty-first centuries, absentee landowners used the flight strip to access their landholdings. Indeed, the jet fuel station at the site was installed in 1979 to store fuel for one landowner's charter jet. In terms of socialization, the nearby Dell Airport Bar was a popular meeting place for dancing and other social events in the late 1940s and 1950s—without the airstrip, this rendezvous locale wouldn't have existed.

Newspaper references to the Dell Flight Strip are infrequent in the postwar years, but it is clear that the rural airport was significant to Dell's economy. Within a few years of the end of the war, the *Dillon Daily Tribune* ran an advertisement from Beaverhead Flying Service offering flying lessons at the flight strip for "anyone flying under the GI Bill or privately." Boy Scout groups frequently met at the flight strip to climb aboard private aircraft for free rides around the upper Beaverhead Valley. Evidence also suggests that the flight strip was a popular landing spot for hunters and anglers. In May 1948, the Butte *Montana Standard* reported that pilots and passengers from Montana, Idaho and Utah had to wait their turn to land at the Dell air strip on opening day of fishing season. From the runway's tie-down area, they walked a mile to the Beaverhead River to try their luck at angling. The average monthly total for pilots landing at the Dell Flight Strip is fifty airplanes; it is more in the summer and hunting season months.

The airport served as a base for search-and-rescue operations on at least two occasions in 1957. In March of that year, five people from Dillon—an attorney and his wife and daughter and a Dillon automobile dealer and his son—perished in a small plane crash near Monida Pass, north of Dillon. The Dell Flight Strip served as an operational base, in addition to the Dillon Airport, hosting a search party, equipment and gasoline trucks to refuel search planes. July of the same year witnessed a spray plane, a converted navy torpedo bomber, out of Dell that went down in the Beaverhead National Forest. The exact circumstances of the crash remain unknown, but the pilot was spraying for spruce budworms under contract to the Forest Service. Initially, all searchers could find was a brain-spattered crash helmet and part of the pilot's jaw. In April 1965, a Dell-area pilot took off from the flight strip in his private plane destined for Ogden, Utah. Soon after, he developed engine trouble and attempted to make it back to the air strip. He "failed to make a successful emergency landing at the Dell airport." The pilot died in the crash. The Civic Aeronautics Board determined that the crash was due to pilot error and inadequate maintenance of the plane. The flight strip does, however, seem to have functioned in the way it was originally intended—as an emergency landing field. An item appeared in an October issue of the *Dillon Examiner* newspaper: "The Leslie McNinches

Nighttime beacons at rural airfields helped guide pilots in for landings during emergencies or inclement weather. The Dell beacon predates the flight strip. *MDT.*

sometimes wish they didn't live so close to the Dell airport especially when a plane comes in for a forced landing like the one did Tuesday."

The Montana Highway Commission retained ownership of the Dell Flight Strip until August 1959, when it turned ownership of it over to the Montana Aeronautics Commission "for administrative purposes." The *Billings Gazette* called the Dell Flight Strip one of the best in Montana. By 1960, the runway had become substantially neglected, with large cracks in the asphalt and weeds growing up through them. Potholes and frayed edges were also significant problems on the runway.

From the 1960s into the 1990s, the Dell Flight Strip was the subject of much discussion among the Aeronautics Commission, Beaverhead County and users of the airport. The slurry seal of the runway was good for only a limited time, and the deterioration of the runway had resumed by the 1970s. While owned by the Aeronautics Commission, it left much of the maintenance of the facility to caretakers. The commission had also begun leasing space to pilots for hangars at an undetermined time. Large cracks once again appeared in the runway with great stands of sweet clover and other weeds growing up in them, making utilizing the runway quite hazardous. In 1977, the commission (now under the aegis of the Montana Department of Commerce) reached an agreement with Beaverhead County to spray the weeds on the runway. The caretaker was responsible for removing the weeds around the lighted delineators, which by this time barely functioned. The caretaker's responsibilities included weed control along the perimeter of the flight strip, replacing burned-out light bulbs on the delineators and reporting when the beacon stopped functioning or when unsafe conditions (i.e., potholes) developed. The flight strip teetered on the verge of abandonment when a "sugar daddy" arrived on the scene and saved it.

In 1988, U.S. Surgical Supply Company executive Leon Hirsch purchased a sheep ranch near Dell. Based in Connecticut, Hirsch flew to his Montana ranch in a chartered Learjet. The Dell Flight Strip, however, was in such poor condition that his pilot was reluctant to land there. To rectify the problem, Hirsch offered to pay for the necessary maintenance and upgrades to the landing field, which included paving the strip in 1989, installing ten-thousand-gallon jet fuel storage tanks and installing the lighted wind cone. Through a series of agreements with the State of Montana, Hirsch took over the operation and maintenance of the flight strip on the condition that it remain open for public use. Weed control remained the responsibility of the county and caretaker. Another paving project occurred in 1997. Improvements to the lighting (excepting the beacon) occurred in 1989 with the rewiring of the lighting system and the upgrade of the bulbs from twenty-five to forty watts. Still, with the repaving projects, it left the tie-down area largely inaccessible because of the steep drop-off from the runway. Problems with livestock and wildlife on the runway resulted in the installation of the enclosing fence in 1990. All these improvements have kept the flight strip open, and in 2019, it handled on average 948 flights per year.

Chapter 23

# NORDEN BOMBSIGHT VAULTS

*g*n 1943, the skies over eastern Montanan were filled with B-17 Flying Fortress bombers. Eastern Montana would play a critical role in the United States' war effort after the country entered World War II in December 1941. The state's wide-open spaces and sparse population made it ideal for the United States Army Air Force (USAAF) to establish training bases for bomber crews. In May 1942, the USAAF established East Base at Great Falls to function as a center for Flying Fortress training and as a stop for ferrying airplanes to the Soviet Union from American factories. It also created three satellite airfields where bomber crews could practice in eastern Montana and western North Dakota. The airfields were located at Cut Bank, Lewistown and Glasgow in northeastern Montana. Each airfield included paved runways long enough to accommodate the bombers, a hangar big enough for the planes, repair shops, barracks, administrative offices, meeting rooms, rec and mess halls and a number of other buildings and structures, along with sewer and water facilities. The bombers began arriving at the airfields in late 1942.

Flying Fortress squadrons trained day and night over a three-month period. They trained every day in varying weather conditions and dropped dummy bombs over six bombing ranges in Montana. Training combined navigation, bombing and gunnery practice with familiarizing crews with all aspects of the B-17 and learning to work together as a team. Four bomb groups trained in the state from 1942 to December 1943. Only one group trained in the state at a time. In Montana, a total of sixteen bomb squadrons trained at the four airfields. With the exception of one squadron, all crews trained in Montana joined the famed Eighth Air Force in northern Europe.

The Norden Bombsight was critical to the Allies' air campaign against Nazi Germany from 1942 to 1945. The bombsight, while not perfect, allowed for the precision bombing of enemy targets from altitudes up to twenty-five thousand feet. The design of the bombsight was a closely guarded military secret, and the USAAF took great pains to protect that secret from Axis spies. All the squadrons based at satellite airfields in Montana trained with the Norden Bombsight in the clear air of eastern Montana and western North Dakota. That training enabled the Allies to successfully bomb German munitions plants, aircraft factories, railroad marshaling yards and other strategic targets inside the Third Reich, eventually contributing to an Allied victory in May 1945.

Because of the bombsight's top-secret status, the secure storage of what was essentially an early analog computer was vital to the Allied war effort. Constructed of reinforced concrete, the storage vaults had eight-inch-thick walls and were impervious to bombs and other explosive devices. Army technicians accessed the bombsight storage rooms through a single steel vault door. The buildings were in isolated areas of the airfield complexes and were surrounded by woven wire fences topped by barbed wire. Sentries, stationed in sentry boxes by the front gate, guarded the structures twenty-four hours a day. In addition, lights on all four sides of the structure prevented any furtive approach to the structure. The strict security that surrounded the Norden Bombsight prevented its theft by enemy spies. The surviving Norden Bombsight storage vaults at the Lewistown and Glasgow airfields well represent those security measures.

Developed in the early 1930s by Dutch immigrant Carl Norden, the Norden Bombsight was one of the most important secret weapons developed by the U.S. military before the Manhattan Project. A complicated early computer, it consisted of a system of gyroscopes, gears and optics that could, at least theoretically, "place a single bomb in a pickle barrel from 20,000 feet." The U.S. Navy began tests on the bombsight in 1935, and the U.S. Army contracted to purchase ninety thousand bombsights at $1.5 billion from the New York City–based Carl I. Norden, Inc. company in 1937. The gyroscope-stabilized instrument computed drift and dropping angle for bombs after data was entered into the machine, including ground speed, air resistance and the estimated time of the fall of the bombs. Although his wife reputedly called him the "Merchant of Death," Norden intended the bombsight to allow for precision, high-altitude bombing that would inflict a maximum damage on military targets with minimum harm to civilians and private property.

Despite his best intentions, Norden's bombsight was neither very accurate nor discriminating to targets on the ground. Optimum use of the bombsight required a level platform, clear skies over the target and consistent speed on the part of the airplane. When the bomber was under attack from fighter planes and antiaircraft fire from the ground, pilots tended to take evasive action, which diminished the effectiveness of the bombsight. Even in the clear, cloudless skies of the American West during training exercises, the Norden Bombsight was not terribly accurate. In the hazy, cloudy skies of northern Europe, it would prove to be even less so. By early 1943, however, the bombsight's coupling with the B-17 and B-24 bombers' autopilot and a change in tactics developed by General Curtis LeMay of the Eighth Air Force would make the Norden Bombsight more effective, but not to the level advocated by its inventor. Despite the problems with the Norden Bombsight, it remained in service with the USAAF and

Concrete storage vaults housed the top-secret Norden Bombsight, one of America's most closely guarded secrets during World War II. *Montana State Historic Preservation Office.*

the U.S. Navy until the end of the war. The U.S. Air Force used variations of the bombsight until the Vietnam War.

Because the military classified the Norden Bombsight as top-secret, the USAAF made provisions to secure it when not in use. The Lewistown and Glasgow Army Airfield storage vaults are second-generation storage facilities placed in use after the USAAF reclassified them from secret to restricted. Original Norden Bombsight storage facilities consisted of wooden storage buildings with five or six interior concrete storage vaults. Government contractors constructed the bombsight vaults in Lewistown and Glasgow from standardized plans, and they are of the same dimensions. They display poured concrete roofs, identical footprints and surface features. Air crews stored the bombsights in one-half of the vaults on shelving, while the other half of the building functioned as an equipment storage and repair. The history of the 390th Bomb Group described the storage vault: "In the relative secrecy of the bombsight vault, [technicians] worked night and day to ensure the accuracy of the Group's attacks." The USAAF assigned seventy Norden Bombsights to the 390th. Bombardiers checked the bombsights prior to use and installed them in the plexiglass noses of their airplanes. When the bombsights' use was completed, the bombardiers placed them in bags and returned them to the storage facilities. Repair and maintenance technicians for the bombsights were also stationed at the training airfields.

The Norden Bombsight storage vaults at the Lewistown and Glasgow Army Airfields were utilized until 1944, when the USAAF ceased conducting bomber training there. The vault at the Lewistown Airfield is currently used for storage, while the Glasgow vault has been long abandoned. Both are nondescript and rare reminders of the important role Montana played in World War II.

# Chapter 24
# MONTANA WAYSIDES

## THE HIGHWAY REST AREAS

*T*aking a break from driving is an important part of any road trip. In the late nineteenth-century American West, rest stops could be few and far between. Sometimes it meant getting out of a cramped and overcrowded stagecoach and stretching your legs for a bit at a stage station. A privy was then, as it is now, an indispensable commodity. With the arrival of automobiles in the early twentieth century, however, taking a break by the side of the road changed with the technology. A rest area meant a convenient bush or tree. For many, it was a place where you threw out a couple of sleeping bags and spent the night within a few yards of the highway. Local businesses encouraged motorists to stop in their communities and take advantage of the services they had to offer, including tourist cabin camps or campgrounds. Stops in rural areas were left to the whims of the drivers and their passengers.

In the early 1930s, the MDT developed roadside picnic and camping areas where motorists could stop, take a break and spend some quality time communing with Montana's great outdoors. The picnic areas were primitive, consisting of only a couple of picnic tables, a trash receptacle and, perhaps, a historical marker and a fire pit. In 1934, the department took the concept one step further and built its first rest area in Helena. The first official highway rest area was located at the junction of North Last Chance Gulch, then a part of U.S. Highway 91, and U.S. Highway 10 (now Lyndale Avenue) in Helena across from Memorial Park. It included an information center, drinking fountain, picnic tables and a circular stone parking structure.

The rest area was located amid a beautifully landscaped strip park that its designers intended to hide the city dump from the highway. It was the only rest area of its kind in Montana during the Great Depression. While the Montana Highway Department built other roadside beautification areas near urban areas in the state, the North Last Chance Gulch site was the only one to specifically include amenities for motorists.

During the summer of 1933, the highway department began the reconstruction of Highway 91 between Helena and Sieben. The project included the construction of two railroad overpasses on North Last Chance Gulch. The department planned to pave North Last Chance Gulch from the railroad overpasses south to the intersection of Neill Avenue in downtown Helena. The highway between the overpasses and West Lyndale Avenue was, however, one of the most unsightly stretches of road in southwestern Montana—the city dump was located on the west side of the highway in plain view of all who traveled the highway as it entered the state's Capital City.

In the early days of President Franklin Roosevelt's New Deal, the federal government looked for ways to put men to work on public works projects. State highway departments were the benefactors of much of this federal bounty, as building roads and bridges proved an excellent way to spend federal money and provide relief to the states' unemployed. Although much of the work was accomplished through the regular highway programs, there were other avenues available for the highway departments to employ men through force account projects without going through the regular bidding process. One way was building roadside beautification or other improvement projects.

In 1934, the highway department began a new program to construct strip parks as beautification projects next to federal aid highways in urban areas. The federal Bureau of Public Roads supported the program, which allocated $40,000 for the projects in Montana. Plans consisted of landscaping, planting trees and the construction of parking areas with drinking fountains. It was also the intent of the program's developers to construct the sites where they could provide buffers between the highways and areas blighted by urban industrial development. The highway department chose four sites for the program in Montana: Helena, Great Falls, Missoula and Butte. The department hired Great Falls superintendent of parks and landscape architect Thomas S.M. Lease to manage the program; he was given the title of "landscape engineer."

The first beautification project occurred near the Sixth Street Underpass in Great Falls. The project included landscaping but not the construction of a parking area. The remaining three beautification projects were funded through a highway department force account in early April 1934 in Missoula, Butte and Helena. The highway commission included the Helena project in the plans for the paving project between Neill Avenue and the railroad overpasses on North Last Gulch/U.S. Highway 91. Lease completed the landscaping plans in March and specified the construction of a park along the west side of the roadway between West Lyndale Avenue and the southernmost overpass over the Great Northern Railway tracks. The one-hundred-foot-wide park included planting birch, willow, spruce, poplar, fir and mountain ash trees and a circular stone parking area and water fountain. The City of Helena, in conjunction with this project, built a new city park on the east side of the highway, now called Memorial Park. The city also provided water to the highway department's park on the west side of the road. The highway department provided $6,000 for the beautification project, which would be built by local men obtained through the local National Re-employment Office.

A work crew began on the Helena project in April 1934 with a force of three men. Lease's original design for the Helena site included the construction of a circular stone parking area and a water fountain. The BPR was, to say the least, unimpressed with Lease's design. The bureau's district engineer, William Lynch, stated that the parking area was not efficient as a parking space and that aesthetically, a round structure did not "fit" the straight lines of the adjacent roadway. Lynch suggested that Lease incorporate a rectangular layout for the parking area, as a rounded one would "not conveniently park more than 20 cars at the most."

Lynch's recommendations incensed Lease. In a lengthy reply written to the district engineer the day before the project was completed, Lease defended his choice of parking structure. After considering the "relative merits" of a square, rectangular and circular area, he opted for something that was nearly "fool proof"—the circular structure. Lease had little faith in Helena's drivers. After closely observing them for several weeks, he noted, "My observation of the parking habits of the people in this vicinity shows that the first car into such a rectangular parking area will invariably park as his fancy strikes him, instead of as he theoretically should. Thus, when half a dozen or so cars are parked, they usually are so placed that the next man has to do some figuring to get parked at all."

Lease intended to place signs reading, "'Head your car into the wall,' or something to that effect," around the exterior of the structure. He concluded, "I agree that the rectangular parking area is far more efficient theoretically,

Highway rest areas were a new concept in the 1930s. The first provided only parking, a drinking fountain, picnic tables and attractive landscaping. *MDT.*

and would have been more in keeping with the planting project as a whole, yet when the human factor is considered, I believe that the circular parking area in this place has its merits." Finally, Lease reminded Lynch that the stone parking area was not the main point of the project. That was the creation of a roadside park that would screen the city dump from the highway.

Not all the vegetation planted in the new roadside park could be obtained from local nurseries, so the workers took some "from natural locations in the adjacent hillsides." Prominent local stonemason Joe Merzlock constructed the circle for a cost of $377. He used 106 sacks of cement for the footings and mortar. The stone probably came from the dredge tailings located just north of the park. The circle had a capacity of thirty automobiles and a gravel parking surface. Work on the beautification project was completed in early June 1934.

Through the efforts of Bob Fletcher, the head of the department's tourism programs, a contractor erected a log building at the corner of North Main and West Lyndale at the south end of the new park. The father of Montana's tourism programs in the 1930s, Fletcher intended the cabin to function as an information center for tourists. He was a firm believer that all tourism-related facilities must promote Montana's frontier past, look rustic and be staffed by uniformed, courteous, well-mannered young men. The building was the first of many log cabin port of entry stations and local highway department–sponsored museums that dotted the state's landscape in the 1930s and '40s. When construction began on the National Guard Armory in 1940, the department relocated the cabin. It eventually ended up on Eleventh Avenue near the intersection of Lamborn Street, where it now houses an antique store.

The park on North Last Chance Gulch was one of the first planned highway rest areas in Montana. Like today's interstate rest areas, the highway department intended the site to provide a pleasant place for motorists to get out of their cars, stretch their legs and enjoy a pleasant setting. Information was available for tourists who planned to visit the Capital City and its surrounding area. Although eventually bypassed by Interstate 15 in 1962, this early highway rest area remained an effective buffer between the roadway and the city landfill until the construction of the YMCA and Centennial Park. In 2002, the MDT dismantled the stone circle and moved it a short distance to the west to accommodate a street-widening project. The landscaping largely remains, however, and the circle now encloses the pole for a large American flag.

With the federal government's initiation of the Interstate Highway Program, the highway department adopted the American Association of State Highway Officials guidelines, *A Policy on Safety Rest Areas for the National System of Interstate and Defense Highways*, in 1958. The rules outlined how roadside safety rest areas would be incorporated into the newly created interstate highway system. They provided guidance on rest area amenities, such as restrooms, picnic tables, trash receptacles, drinking fountains and, where warranted, telephone booths. The guidelines also specified a general site configuration. Under the plan, rest areas would be built concurrently with interstate projects. This simple idea, however, took on a life of its own as visionaries looked beyond the basic guidelines and saw an "opportunity to reconnect people with the places they were traveling through," thus providing an identifier for the state or region. The highway department adopted the policy in 1961 and modified it over the next few years to include Montana's two-lane primary routes.

The Montana Highway Department began building rest areas in 1962. Over the next decade, it constructed thirty-one interstate and primary route rest areas, including eleven interstate and non-interstate rest areas in 1966 alone. The *Billings Gazette* called it a "blossoming system of roadside rest areas" designed for the "weary traveler to relax in the shade, have a picnic lunch and perhaps even grab a few winks before resuming the journey." Each rest area featured a main building with running water and "flush-type toilets," electricity, picnic tables, benches and trash cans. The highway department prohibited overnight camping at the sites. Highway maintenance crews were responsible for the custodial work, while the agency contracted with local citizens to empty trash cans and monitor the facilities.

When the highway department adopted its rest area plan, there were already ninety-two rest areas along the highways in the state. These included rest stops developed and maintained by the U.S. Forest Service and many roadside picnic areas built by the department in the 1930s. In October 1962, the MDT hired a landscape architect, William Schweyen, to develop a standard landscape design for the department's new rest areas. A 1966 article in the highway department's newsletter, the *Center Line*, stated that Schweyen attempted to blend each rest area into the surrounding scenery, with only the restroom buildings being of the same design for each rest stop. By the end of the year, the department and the Bureau of Public Roads had identified the locations of the proposed new rest areas. These "little [sanctuaries] for weary motorists" would be located every fifty miles along the interstates and at scenic locations along the primary routes.

By 1966, nineteen rest areas were in various stages of completion, with eleven completed that year. Each of the new rest areas was landscaped with grasses, shrubs and trees, and each exhibited its own "individual flair" with landscaping specific to that site. Picnic tables, some with shelters, stood near the restroom buildings. Only the restroom buildings displayed a uniform design. The *Center Line* described the basic idea for the rest area sites:

> *The unique semi-circle design of each rest area building is trademark of Montana. Inside the stout buildings are modern flush-type facilities and wash basins. A drinking fountain is attached to the outside of the building. The entire structure is engineered for low maintenance and a minimum of vandalism. All pipes, gauges and machinery are shielded behind locked doors and fixtures inside the buildings are kept to a minimum.*

Outside lights automatically turned on at dusk and remained on until dawn. Highway department road plans engineer Melvin Wickman boasted that the intent of each rest area was to "provide small pockets of beauty along our highway, in which weary motorists can rest in peace." The first interstate rest area opened on Interstate 15, about midway through the Wolf Creek canyon, in 1966. As of 2020, sixty-four rest areas and truck parking areas have been strung along the highways, pearls of rest, relaxation

Today's rest areas are modern affairs that feature up-to-date amenities designed to give motorists a break from the highway. *MDT.*

and a break from the road. True to the original designers' vision, the rest area system is undergoing a renaissance with innovative and modern new restroom designs that are more security-conscious and user friendly, ADA accessible and visually stunning—truly a big improvement over a dilapidated log cabin or a lone bush on an empty prairie.

## Chapter 25

# LIKE TWO NEW DIMES IN THE SKY

## NICK MARIANA AND THE
## GREAT MONTANA FLYING SAUCER FILM

*F*or some, fame comes unexpectedly and sometimes lasts a lifetime, but not for the reasons they hoped. Sometimes it's just a matter of being in the right place at the right time—with a good camera. For Nick Mariana, it came in the form of a sixteen-second movie he shot in the parking lot of the Legion Ball Park in Great Falls, Montana. The film showed two alleged unidentified flying objects (UFOs) as they soared behind the water tower of the General Mills grain complex on 25th Street North. The footage, possibly the first to capture the images of flying saucers on motion picture film, defined Mariana for the rest of his life. The grainy film footage is legendary in UFO lore and has yet to be scientifically explained. Who knows, it may actually be what Mariana and his supporters claimed it to be—the images of two alien spacecraft.

Born in Miles City in August 1913, Nick Mariana graduated from the University of Montana in 1937. He married Claretta Dunn in 1939 and served in the U.S. Army Air Force at East Base (later Malmstrom Air Force Base) in Great Falls during World War II. A huge baseball fan and promoter, Mariana organized a base baseball team and wrote for the base newspaper. That enthusiasm for local sports carried over after the war. In 1948, the Great Falls Baseball Club hired him as general manager of the pioneer baseball league team the Selectrics. In addition to his managerial duties, he worked as a sports official, sportscaster and scout for farm clubs for the Brooklyn Dodgers and Minnesota Twins. Definitely an extrovert, he was also a popular speaker at local civic club functions.

Late in the morning of August 15, 1950, Mariana was climbing the steps to his office at the Legion Ball Park when he looked north across the Missouri River toward the Anaconda Company copper refinery in Black Eagle. He often looked at the smoke coming from the refinery stacks to gauge which direction the wind was blowing A flash caught his eye, and he saw two objects hovering and spinning over the smokestack. Mariana later reported that they looked like two new dimes in the sky. When they began to move to the south, Mariana raced back down the steps to retrieve a new sixteen-millimeter movie camera he had in the glove compartment of his car. From the parking lot of the ballpark, he called for his secretary, Virginia Raunig, to come out of their office to witness what he was observing. Mariana was able to retrieve his handheld camera from his car and shoot about sixteen seconds of film before the objects disappeared into the clear blue sky southeast of Great Falls. Mariana sent the film to an out-of-state photo laboratory for processing and reported it to both of the city's newspapers, the *Great Falls Tribune* and the *Great Falls Leader*.

At the time of the sighting, central Montana was flooded by reports of mysterious objects in the sky. For several weeks after he filmed the objects, Mariana showed the film to local civic and sports organizations before he submitted it to the air force for further study. The air force provided two contradictory explanations of the film: first, that it was too dark to see anything, and second, that the objects shown on the film were not weather balloons but probably two F-94 Starfire fighter jets known to be in the vicinity of the sighting. Allegations of a government coverup began when the air force returned the footage to Mariana—minus two feet of film that purportedly showed the objects hovering over the smelter. According to Mariana, the missing footage was the most important part of the film because it showed the objects in clear detail compared to what was on the eight feet of film returned to him.

For years, charges about the missing film footage flew between Mariana and the air force, leading to a claim by one UFO researcher that the military forced Mariana from his job as the general manager of the Selectrics in 1953, gave him a $10,000 check and promised him a government job if he stopped making the allegations against the air force. The claim is patently false; Mariana enthusiastically promoted the film until his death in 1999. He even appeared in a low-budget semi-documentary motion picture, titled *Unidentified Flying Objects*, telling viewers the story behind his film. The film was the first to

Nick Mariana played a significant role in the 1956 motion picture *UFO: Unidentified Flying Objects*. It was the first national exposure of Mariana's film. *Author's collection.*

show the Montana Film, as it had become known, to a nationwide audience—which sparked renewed public and official interest in it.

Described by government investigators as a "reliable trustworthy individual [who] is highly respected in the community," Mariana believed he had filmed two UFOs and defended his reputation and the film for decades. In 1950, he even sued *Cosmopolitan* magazine after it published an article titled "The Disgraceful Flying Saucer Hoax." Although the author concluded that Mariana had made an honest mistake when he filmed the jets, Mariana felt that the article depicted him as a "liar, a prankster, half-wit, crank, publicity hound, and fanatic" and that he fabricated the film to "play on the gullibility and apprehension of the average citizen." He eventually lost the $25,000 libel suit—but not his advocacy of the film.

Periodically during the 1950s and '60s, the air force, the CIA, government investigators and UFO enthusiasts interviewed Mariana about his film and what he saw that day in August 1950. Although the CIA blew it off as the two F-94s, other investigators could not come to a consensus about what the film actually showed. They were not the reflections of birds, weather balloons or meteors. They might have been the jets, but more than one investigator said no, they were moving too fast and seemed to be generating their own light. After over seventy years, the sighting is still listed as an unknown.

The jury on the Montana Movie is still out, but one thing is certain: Great Falls was, for a time, one of the UFO capitals of the world. Within weeks of Mariana's sighting, the city's newspapers reported sightings of flying cigars, glowing bananas, orbs and a flaming sky-borne tumbleweed. The *Great Falls Tribune* tended to pooh-pooh the reports when it editorialized about "the good old days when the only objects that filled Montana skies were an occasional goose and a jet or two." But with the installation of nuclear-tipped Intercontinental Ballistic Missiles in the surrounding area, the mission of Malmstrom Air Force Base changed in the 1960s to one decidedly more deadly. Concurrently, the frequency of UFO sightings increased—and generated more official interest. Over the years, hundreds of sightings have been reported in the Great Falls area. Many believe that it is because of the missile installations. In January 2008, the city's pioneer baseball team (once known as the Selectrics) changed its name from the White Sox to the Voyagers. Great Falls Baseball Club officials introduced the team's new space age logo in a high-tech multimedia presentation that included a video depiction of Mariana's UFO sighting. Club president Vinney Purpura said the new name would "relate to our city, or events that occurred in our city." Like it or not, skeptic or believer, the Montana Film has become a recognized part of Great Falls history. Nick Mariana would be proud.

Chapter 26

# ONE OF A KIND

## THE PUGSLEY BRIDGE

*I*n addition to being the Last Best Place, Montana is also home to many one-of-a-kind historic sites—some of which we take for granted. Many of these places are in the more remote places of the state and are not widely known to most people. The Dearborn River High Bridge southwest of Augusta may be the last remaining pin-connected half-deck truss bridge in the United States. That's why the MDT rehabilitated and preserved the span at the beginning of the twenty-first century. One structure in north-central Montana literally stands out as the only one of its kind in the United States and perhaps even the world. The Pugsley Bridge is a unique cable stay bridge built in the remote badlands south of Chester in Liberty County. To say there are no others like it is an understatement.

The concept of cable stay bridges has been known by engineers since the late sixteenth century, but they were not widely used until the nineteenth century, and that was mostly in Europe. The design gained popularity largely because of the European Industrial Revolution, when iron and steel became more widely available to builders. Cable stay bridges are different from suspension bridges in that the cables run directly from the towers to the deck. On suspension bridges, the cables hang between the towers with cables suspended between the cables and the deck. Early suspension bridges, like the Brooklyn Bridge, though, feature both cable stay and suspension characteristics. Cable stay bridges are optimal for structures that are longer than cantilever structures and shorter than suspension bridges. Built in 1890, the oldest remaining cable stay bridge in the nation is the Dale suspension bridge at Bluff Dale, Texas.

Cable stay bridges look a lot like suspension bridges. For years, many folks mistakenly believed the Pugsley Bridge to be a suspension bridge. The towers are the primary load-bearing structures for cable stay bridges. They transmit the dead weight (the deck structure) and the live loads (traffic) to the ground. For cable stay bridges, ground anchorages are not usually required, but the Pugsley Bridge has cables anchored by concrete block "deadmen" that provide additional support for the towers. Likewise, cable stay structures typically don't have vertical cables descending from the main cables to the deck. The Pugsley Bridge does have that feature, which was incorporated into the structure by the bridge's designer, Tom Hurdle. This distinguishes this bridge from a standard cable stay structure. The innovative bridge design allowed Hurdle to keep within the limited county budget available to him. The Pugsley Bridge may very well be the first cable stay bridge built in the United States in the mid-twentieth century and the only one of this design.

While popular in Europe, cable stay bridges never really caught on in the United States, and by the turn of the twentieth century, they had largely fallen from favor. Indeed, popular bridge design instruction manuals, such as J.A.L. Waddell's *Bridge Engineering* (1916), do not even mention the type. At the end of World War II, however, the expansion of the United States highway system and the availability of cheaper materials and larger construction machinery significantly lowered the price to build cable stay bridges. The first major post–World War II cable stay bridge is the 1,089-foot Strömsund Bridge in Strömsund, Sweden, built in 1956. In the United States, the O'Connell Bridge in Sitka, Alaska, is the first major cable stay bridge in the United States (1972). The O'Connell Bridge is 1,350 feet in length. The Pugsley Bridge predates both structures.

During the early spring of 1947, an ice jam moved an old steel truss bridge located at the site of the current span off its foundation and onto the riverbank about a half mile downstream. The Liberty County commissioners hired the Billings-based R.T. Hurdle and Sons engineering firm to estimate the cost of placing the old bridge back onto its foundation. The company reckoned that it would cost the county $53,520 to complete the work. The county held a bond election in July 1948 to raise funds to repair the old bridge. But before the work could begin, a second ice jam in 1949 moved the bridge another mile downstream and all but demolished it.

Because the destruction of the old bridge ended any chances for rehabilitation, the county and engineer Tom Hurdle made plans to construct a new bridge at the site. Hurdle decided on a cable stay bridge design, as

Tom Hurdle's unique cable stay bridge best accommodated the severe site conditions of the Marias River breaks in north-central Montana. *Kristi Hager photo, MDT.*

it would provide a clear span across the Marias River and minimize the potential damage to the structure from future ice jams. Liberty County advertised for bids to construct the new bridge, but all came in much higher than the engineer's estimate, and the commissioners rejected them. Instead of relying on a contractor, the county commissioners decided to use county forces to build the new bridge under the supervision of Tom Hurdle's younger brother Willard. Liberty County forces began work on the new bridge in September 1949. The builders did not use falsework to construct the new bridge, and they incorporated portions of the original structure (i.e., the abutments and one of the approach piers) into the design of the structure. The county employed only eight men on the job, with construction equipment consisting of a backhoe, a "concrete mixer, 2-drum hoist…winch truck, compressor and welding and burning equipment."

The Great Falls Iron Works Company supplied the structural steel for the bridge. The cables were provided by the Pacific Wire Rope Company of Los Angeles and the timber by the Larraine Valley Lumber Company of Cottage Creek, Oregon. The county completed work on the bridge in July 1950. The structure cost $51,546, nearly $2,000 less than the engineer's

The Pugsley Bridge employs a distinctive system of cables to support the sweeping deck of the structure. *Kristi Hager photo, MDT.*

estimate and the cost of the bond. That R.T. Hurdle and Sons was proud of the bridge was demonstrated on the company's stationery—it included a profile of the Pugsley Bridge.

In 1963, problems surfaced regarding the camber (arch) of the bridge deck. It had settled significantly because the cables had overstretched. Tom Hurdle believed it was because of overloading when the U.S. Bureau of Reclamation constructed nearby Tiber Dam in the 1950s. The bridge also suffered from a deteriorated deck, and the timber guardrails were in poor condition. By 1967, the problems had not been rectified, and Hurdle contacted Montana representative Arnold Olsen to acquire federal funds for the repair of the bridge. Olsen's bid for federal funds failed, and it was not until 1973 that any work was done on the bridge. That year, Liberty County removed the original timber deck and asphalt overlay and replaced it with a corrugated metal deck. In the mid-1980s, the MDT removed the corrugated metal deck and replaced it with a timber deck. The agency also removed the original wood guardrails and replaced them with the existing steel I-beam and cable rails.

The Pugsley Bridge's towers stand in stark contrast to the relative flatness of the northern Great Plains. It is a testimonial to the ingenuity of its designer and of Liberty County for supporting its construction. The bridge continues to serve local ranchers, farmers and recreationalists. Some may wonder about it now, but at the time of its construction, it was hailed as a marvel, a one-of-a-kind structure in the wilds of northern Montana.

# Chapter 27

# COLD WAR OUTPOSTS

## THE MONTANA RADAR STATIONS

One of the most enduring images of the American West is the U.S. Cavalry charging out of Fort Apache to rescue besieged settlers from hostile Indians. While the image is not entirely accurate, military posts played an important role in protecting people from the dangers associated with living on a remote frontier and, in the process, became important to the communities they protected. The federal government established its last post in Montana, Fort Harrison outside Helena, in 1892, not so much to protect the city's citizens from the state's First Citizens but to provide a military presence in the state. The last of the fort's soldiers departed the post during World War II, and it became a facility to treat veterans of the world wars, Korean, Vietnam and, recently, those who served in the War on Terror.

Almost a century after the end of the Indian wars, however, the military returned to the northern Great Plains and established the modern equivalent of the old frontier outpost. Over the course of nine years, from 1952 to 1961, the U.S. Air Force established a network of radar installations and air bases in Montana designed to protect the country and its allies from the threat of a sneak attack from the Soviet Union. Instead of rifles, bugles and sabers, however, the military utilized the latest in radar and computer technologies to weave an electronic radar web over North America. Montana's wide-open spaces, sparse population and location on the anticipated flight path from the Soviet Union over the Arctic made the state prime real estate for the military during the Cold War as it sought ways to prevent a nuclear attack on the American heartland.

After the Soviet Union's detonation of an atomic bomb in 1949 and the beginning of the Korean War the following year, tensions mounted between the United States and the USSR. To deter a communist attack, the air force established a radar network to protect American airspace. Using the most sophisticated computer and radar technology available, dedicated air force officers and airmen manned the stations in some of the most isolated places in the country. The radar system, though, was not complete, and there were vast gaps where Soviet planes might conceivably mount an attack. To plug the gaps, the air force, concurrent with the early radar system, created the Ground Observer Corps to supplement the electronic screen. It relied, however, on civilian sky watchers and was only a temporary solution until the radar technology improved to where it could carry the entire load.

The United States and Canada activated the radar net shortly after 1949. Based at stations scattered over Montana, the Dakotas, Minnesota and western Canada, the radar could detect Soviet bombers and report that information to air bases, like Malmstrom Air Force Base at Great Falls, which would then scramble fighters to intercept them. The stations employed the most up-to-date technology of the time and fed the information into analog computer systems through telephone lines, which could analyze the probable targets. Montana was on the front line of the Cold War from the very beginning, yet the radar stations are an almost forgotten chapter of the state's history.

The U.S. Air Force built some of the nation's first Cold War radar installations in Montana. Beginning in 1952, the air force established seven radar stations across the state from Kalispell in the northwest to Miles City in the southeast, including bases near Cut Bank, Havre, Great Falls, Lewistown and Opheim. The stations were manned by Aircraft Control and Warning (AC&W) squadrons consisting of 100 to 250 military and civilian workers. The self-contained military communities were little towns unto themselves. They included administrative and support facilities as well as communications, recreational, supply buildings and quarters for single and married airmen and officers. These all clustered around the stations' three radomes, fiberglass geodesic structures designed to protect the sensitive radar equipment from the harsh Montana weather. The stations each had a range of around three hundred miles and were electronically tied into other AC&W posts by microwave relay stations and telephone lines. Initially, it was all vacuum tube technology until the first solid state transistorized digital computers went online in 1961. There were also nine small automated "gap filler" stations scattered across the state. With the range of only sixty-five miles, the air force placed them where enemy aircraft could fly low enough to avoid detection.

One of the most typical of the radar stations was established in 1954 in the badlands about eight miles west of Miles City. The 902nd AC&W Squadron radar station guarded the United States from that lonely outpost for fourteen years until closing in 1968. As with the frontier posts of the nineteenth century, living in the middle of nowhere presented its own challenges. Nature constantly intruded on the station with scorching hot summers and brutally cold winters. Gumbo roads made travel difficult during the spring thaw and during the downpours of the summer. Rattlesnakes were a common sight sunning themselves on the concrete walkways or, occasionally, inside the living quarters. Black widow spiders far outnumbered the number of people living at the station. Indeed, one bored airman stationed there spent his off-duty hours raising the deadly arachnids in the enlisted men's quarters. The "soda water" from the station's wells made laundering difficult, and water had to be hauled to the station in garbage cans from Miles City.

When the specialized electronic equipment broke down, the station's remoteness made replacing it a challenge, especially during the winter months. Along with rattlesnakes and technical glitches, the radar station also had to contend with local residents who did not always understand military protocol. One former station maintenance person remembered one night when a drunken rancher unknowingly drove his pickup through the main gate of the station, roared through the middle of the compound and exited it over the helipad at the other end of the site.

Many airmen took second jobs in Miles City or worked part time at one of the nearby ranches to supplement their military pay. Miles City residents welcomed the air force and invited airmen into their homes during the holidays and on other special occasions, forging a close relationship between civilians and military personnel. The same would be true for other radar stations located close enough to communities. For years, the squadron participated in Miles City's Fourth of July celebrations and other community events. One man who was stationed there in the late 1950s remembered marching in Miles City's annual Bucking Horse sale parade and losing "the best unit award to a group of eight to ten-year-old baton twirlers." School-age children of airmen and officers at the Wild Horse radar station north of Havre played on baseball and basketball teams in the city.

Needless to say, the men and women living at the radar station felt they were part of the community outside the confines of the stations. Not a few airmen married local women and moved back to Montana when they had completed their tours of duty. The story of the 902nd AC&W was without doubt repeated across Montana.

The Wild Horse radar station was located about thirty miles northwest of Havre. Established in 1952, it was the home of the 778th AC&W Squadron, whose unit patch showed the caricature of an airman looking at a radar screen and waving at a passing jet. The station's four radars tracked both friendly and enemy aircraft, feeding the data to the control center at Malmstrom Air Force Base in Great Falls. With the advent of nuclear warhead–armed Intercontinental Ballistic Missiles in the 1960s, the station soon became obsolete. The Wild Horse station then functioned as a component of the BUIC II and III system that served as a backup in case the Malmstrom direction center was rendered inoperative. The air force closed the Havre radar station in 1979. For a few years, it served as a NORAD electronic bomb scoring site before closing permanently in 1986, the last such facility to shut down in the state.

Through technological advancements, the personnel at the radar stations remained vigilant and kept track of air traffic, including an occasional U-2 spy plane. In 1961, the air force connected all the radar stations to the Semi-Automatic Ground Environment (SAGE) system, one of the most advanced and successful large digital computer systems ever developed. The result was an automated system that could track and dispatch interceptors to deal with intruders much faster than the old analog system that relied on telephone lines to relay information to the control centers at the Malmstrom and Glasgow air bases.

Despite the addition of SAGE, the radar stations fast became obsolete in the 1960s. Though they could accurately track enemy aircraft, intercontinental ballistic missiles were a different story. Instead of having minutes to react for airplanes, air force personnel had only seconds for missiles. Improvements in technology and the increasing demands of the Vietnam War spelled the end for most of North America's AC&W radar stations by 1970. Three of Montana's stations, including the one near Miles City, closed by 1968. The Opheim and Havre stations remained open until 1979 before they, too, were deactivated and closed. Two facilities, south of Kalispell near Lakeside and Wild Horse north of Havre, converted to civilian use. All the gap filler stations had been sacrificed to military budget cuts in 1960.

Today, Montana is littered with the abandoned remains of America's high-tech twentieth-century answer to the old frontier military posts. The men who served at them, however, have strong and mostly good memories of their time in Montana. The Montana Department of Transportation installed historical markers near Miles City and at Havre to commemorate the efforts of the 902nd and 778th AC&W Squadrons in the national defense and the impact they had on the state during the Cold War.

# Chapter 28

# THE DUDE

## BILLINGS'S DUDE RANCHER LODGE

*T*he roadside lodgings industry boomed in the wake of World War II, reaching its peak in the early 1960s when sixty-one thousand motels peppered the American landscape. The dramatic increase in the number of motels occurred as more Americans had the financial wherewithal to purchase new automobiles after the war and the time to take vacations. As more Americans hit the roads to visit national parks, forests and historic sites, the need for roadside accommodations grew simultaneously with the trend. The sizes of the motel complexes also increased and became more accommodating to the mobile population. One thing that remained a constant, however, was that most motels were small mom-and-pop operations, with each motel a representative of the tastes of its owners, who were fully cognizant of what attracted guests. The Dude Rancher Lodge in Billings reflected the interests of its owners, providing tourists a taste of the mythic Old West.

Beginning after 1945, the old cottage court "motels" of the 1920s and '30s increasingly gave way to motor courts. Structured much like cottage courts, the room units were integrated under single rooflines to appear as a single façade or a single building. Most were single-story complexes with long porches on the façades to visually merge the components of the building and provide shelter for motel guests in inclement weather. Many motor courts included coffee shops or restaurants as part of the operation. Motor courts were built in a wide range of architectural styles, with western themes being the most prevalent because of the popularity of the Old West in movies,

The owners of the Dude Rancher, built in 1950, designed the motel to simulate a nineteenth-century cattleman's cabin. *Author's collection.*

radio and television. They were oriented around central courtyards that made them reminiscent of Spanish haciendas or ranch bunkhouses. Many motor courts included swimming pools or playgrounds in the central court. Motor courts became increasingly known as "motels."

In May 1946, Percival and Annabel Goan purchased several city lots to build their dream motel in downtown Billings. They transferred ownership of the property to the Dude Rancher Lodge Corporation in February 1950 to "purchase, lease construct, manage, and operate hotels, motels and other facilities and accommodations for the housing and entertainment of guests." The Goans formed the corporation in April 1949, naming the company to focus on the dude ranching industry. They capitalized the company at $225,000 with Percy and Annabel, along with their sons, William and J. Phillip, and daughter Nancy Goan Dokken holding the preferred stock in the company. Other investors owned 1,500 shares of common stock and consisted of local businessmen and women from the Billings area, including "ranchers, stockmen, retail merchants, wholesalers, bankers, industrialists, insurance agents, doctors, and private investors." Percy and Annabel devised the plan for the building with the Billings architectural firm of Cushing and Tirrell formalizing the plans. In March 1950, the Dude Rancher Lodge Corporation announced plans to the *Billings Gazette* to construct a hotel on the property.

Born in LaGrange, Illinois, on Christmas Day 1890, Percival Sergeant Goan attended local schools before obtaining a degree in engineering from Cornell University. He first visited Billings during a stopover on his way to Yellowstone National Park in 1907. Perhaps seeing the opportunity there, Goan moved to the Magic City in 1915 and opened Goan Motor Company, rumored to be the first Chevrolet dealership in Montana. In 1916, he enlisted in the U.S. Army and served in the Second Infantry on the Mexican border until 1917, when he shipped out to Europe with the American Expeditionary Force. Goan commanded an artillery battery in France during World War I. Upon his discharge, he returned to Billings and resumed management of his auto dealership.

In 1919, Goan formed the Artificial Ice and Cold Storage Company and served as the firm's president until 1952, when he resigned to devote more time to the newly opened Dude Rancher Lodge. In addition to the dealership and cold storage company, Goan was president of NEHI Beverage Company of Billings from 1939 to 1952, was the founder of Blueband Creamery Company in 1928 and was invested in a "number of other corporations." In addition to his many business interests, Goan served as chairman of the chamber of commerce's Industrial Division, vice president of the Billings Chamber of Commerce, president of the Billings Community Chest and Billings Community Concert Association and was a lifelong member of the Rotary Club. Percy Goan obviously had a lot of faith in his town and the opportunities it offered.

Annabel Goan was the daughter of George and Susie Arnott. George came to Montana in 1910 and established ranches in the Judith Basin and Big Hole Basin. He relocated to Billings in 1914 and operated a cattle ranch near the city until his death in December 1925. Annabel was born in Illinois in 1900 and came to Montana with her family. She attended the National Cathedral Girls' School in Washington, D.C., the University of Montana and the University of California–Berkeley. She married Percy Goan in 1920. She served as the president of the Dude Rancher Lodge Corporation from Percy's death in 1962 until 1981. She also managed the motel from 1950 until 1982.

Even before construction on the new motel began, Billings's newspapers reported on the qualities that would set the Dude Rancher Lodge apart from other hostelries in the city. In late 1949 or early 1950, the *Billings Herald* reported that a new and unique hotel would be built in the Magic City. In early March 1950, the *Billings Gazette* and the *Herald* announced that Percy and Annabel Goan would build "a new type of hostelry." Even though the

Cushing and Terrell company had not yet finalized the plans, enough was presented in the newspapers about the establishment to pique the interest of Billings's residents. Details at first concentrated on the exterior, stating that the "general design will follow the lines of early log cabins with a low pitched roof. Horizontal lines will be emphasized." The new motel would have fifty-nine guestrooms along with a lobby, office, lounge and coffee shop. The building would surround a central court with the walls of the motel clad in textured brick and the second floor in red cedar "planking."

The newspapers placed most of the attention on the proposed interior of the Dude Rancher Lodge, especially the décor of the guestroom units. Each one of the rooms, the *Billings Herald* stated, would be dedicated to one of the guest ranches in the Billings vicinity.

> *The brand of the ranch would be burned on the bedroom door and some pieces of furniture. A large picture of the ranch and a framed description of the ranch—its location, facilities, and history, would be hung on the walls. Special dude ranch information would be kept in the office. The Dude Rancher's Association is now considering this program.*

Each room would be heated with hot water heat, and every room would have individually regulated air conditioning units that were "novel in several respects." Ranch-type furniture would be placed in the rooms along with bedspreads and draperies that carried ranch and Indian motifs. The second-floor rooms would be carpeted, and the ground-floor rooms would have tile floors with Navajo-style scatter rugs on the floor. Each room included a closet and full bathroom with shower.

The Billings-based Riedesel Construction Company began construction of the building in mid-April 1950. The Lohoff Brothers Company poured the concrete foundation for the motel. The Goans acquired the "aged... long-weathered" bricks used for the exterior from the recently demolished St. Vincent's Hospital, the Washington Public School and the Russell-Miller Milling Company on 1st Avenue South. Longtime Billings resident Arne Graf did the "rustic" masonry work. Other subcontractors on the project included Christenson Plumbing and Heating Company and Yellowstone Electric Company. The Logan-Leytham Company supplied the casement windows. The Holliday Furniture Company provided the furniture, carpets and mattresses for the motel. A Texas firm manufactured the furniture, while the carpeting was specially made by Hardwick-Magee, a "century old rug firm of Philadelphia." Lamb's Inc. furnished the equipment in the coffee

The interior of the Dude included many unique features, like rope stair rails, pine wood walls and the distinctive carpeting, to evoke the Old West. *Author's collection.*

shop, called the Stirrup. The Dude Rancher Lodge opened for business with an open house on December 17, 1950.

Percy and Annabel Goan intended that the motel not just be a place to stay but also an experience. Like many owner-operated motels of the time, the design and interior decoration of the place reflected the interests of the owners and was also intended to make the establishment one of a kind. Annabel Goan and her daughter Nancy developed the interior decorating scheme at the Dude Rancher Lodge. The interior walls of the motel were paneled in knotty pine and tongue-and-groove doors with $Z$ braces on all the doors. The floors in the lounge, coffee shop and second-floor rooms were carpeted with beige carpets with the images of cattle brands woven into them. Floors on the first-floor room were tile decorated with Navajo-style scatter rugs. Specially made furniture was made of oak and exhibited a mythic Old West feel. All the rooms were furnished with a desk, chairs, floor lamp and bedside table. The beds were eighty inches in length rather than the standard six-foot length and had western-type bed frames and headboards. Drapes in the rooms depicted scenes of Virginia City, Montana, cowboys on bucking broncos, Indian warriors and pictographs copied from the nearby Pictograph Cave site.

The lobby and lounge are located in the north half of the façade section of the building. The specially made beige carpet with the brands of local ranches woven into it was located in the lounge. The lobby was illuminated by large windows on the east and west and also by unique light fixtures, according to the *Billings Herald*:

> *Light shines down from fixtures decorated with hand hammered copper silhouettes which in a series of pictures tell the history of transportation in the West. Starting with the trapper on foot, the prospector with his pack mules and the covered wagon. They progress up to the modern streamlined train and the Stratocruiser.*

The stairs leading to the second floor had large woven rope handrails. The lounge is located to the south of the lobby. It, too, was illuminated by large picture windows and dominated by a fireplace of "mellowed brick." The Goans' purposely kept the lounge small, "giving it an atmosphere of a home." Billings artist LeRoy Greene provided three paintings in the lounge hanging over the fireplace. Display cases were installed between the lounge and lobby. The cases exhibited examples of Indian art and other western artifacts. The lounge held furniture "decorated with hand-carvings of longhorn steer herds, cactus plants, and horseshoes."

The motel's coffee shop, the Stirrup, was, by all accounts, a dining experience. The custom-made carpeting covered the floor, and the furniture consisted of tooled oak with cowhide seats and backs. The pedestals of the counter seats were wrapped with rope. The ceiling light fixtures were similar in design to those in the lobby and consisted of hammered copper with mica lites that depicted "interesting western scenes," including a stagecoach holdup, an Indian dance, a pack train and a dance hall scene. Wall lights were set in horseshoe candelabra that threw a "soft light" on the dining area. Reproductions of Indian spearheads were used on the coat rack.

> *The tableware is branded with the brand of one of the stockholders on the wooden handles. His food is served to him on dishes bearing the design of a roundup chuckwagon scene surrounded with the brands of stockholders around the rim. He drinks from a glass decorated with stirrups. The menu is in the shape of a cowboy hat. He flips the ashes from his cigarette into an ashtray made from mule shoes.*

The coffee shop provided soda fountain service, and the cooking was done in full view of the guests. The Goans specifically touted that the Stirrup would feature home cooking.

The Dude Rancher Lodge was truly a family affair. Percy and Annabel managed the business and served as the president and vice president, respectively, of the Dude Rancher Lodge Corporation. Their children, William and J. Philip Goan and Nancy Dokken, served as the officers in the company and the majority stockholders. Indeed, the Goans promoted the family atmosphere of the motel as much as they did the western theme that ran throughout the operation. The Dude Rancher provided an affordable and welcoming alternative to the hotels in downtown Billings. "The Dude" became a popular hangout for ranchers and farmers visiting the Magic City. According to a motel manager, ranchers and other guests played cards on tables in the Stirrup and the lounge until the early hours of the mornings. Some of the tables used by them still grace those areas. Percy died as a result of injuries sustained in an automobile accident in Wyoming in June 1962. His widow, Annabel, managed the hotel his death. She lived in an apartment behind the front desk until her death in 1983. Rumors that her ghost haunts the Dude Rancher Lodge persist.

In November 1987, the corporation reorganized and increased the number of directors from three to five individuals. Grandson Richard Goan was president of the company, having replaced Annabel as its agent after her death in 1983. Two years later, the directors went outside the company and named attorney Joseph Womack as the corporation's agent. The Dude Rancher Lodge Corporation officially dissolved in July 1992. In 1992, Virginia Carlsen purchased the Dude Rancher Lodge from the Dude Rancher Lodge Corporation. Under Carlsen's ownership, the Dude Rancher Lodge has maintained its Old West and family atmosphere. It is still a popular place to stay for celebrities and vacationers. In 1951, one guest told the *Billings Gazette*, "In Hawaii I immediately wanted to discard my city clothes and dress like the natives in the islands. Here I have the urge to shed my business suit and get into a cowboy outfit. Dude Rancher Lodge has the 'feel' of the Old West." Indeed, the "Spirit of the West is everywhere evident in Dude Rancher Lodge," Billings's most unique motel.

# Chapter 29

# DIAMONDS IN THE ROUGH

## MISS MONTANA HIGHWAYS

*I*n times past, we took certain things for granted that wouldn't be considered appropriate today. For a while, some events at the Montana Department of Transportation were a really big deal that garnered a lot of local attention but then abruptly ended. One of these big deals was the annual Miss Montana Highways contest held at the old Montana Highway Department from 1970 to 1973. The competition spotlighted the department's female employees, and it reveals to us today that most women employed at the department then were clerical workers and secretaries. The intent of Miss Montana Highways was to provide a pretty face for the department at interstate highway dedications and for important social and political functions.

In January 1970, the Montana Highway Department's information officer, Kermit Anderson, announced the first Miss Montana Highways contest. The purpose of the contest was "to elect a comely young woman to represent the Montana State Highway Commission at dedications, open houses, ceremonies, and other functions." The potential winner had to be female (it was clearly specified in the rules), an employee of the department, outgoing and attractive with a "sparkling personality" and "pleasant voice." Candidates were also required to be well versed in the functions of the highway department. Marital status didn't matter—although most candidates were single. While department heads submitted candidates for consideration, they were encouraged to solicit the opinions of their employees about the contestants. Like high school and college elections, supporters campaigned on behalf of their candidates with homemade posters.

Sue Holloran served as the first Miss Montana Highways from 1970 to 1971. She originally worked at the highway department as a clerk-typist. *MDT.*

That first year of the contest, administrators submitted applications to the judges for thirteen women ranging in ages from nineteen to thirty-four. All were employed as stenographers, clerks or typists, and at least two contestants were married. Ten judges (all male), including the state highway engineer, selected the winner. It was definitely a different time, and the content of the

As Miss Montana Highways, Kitty Sullivan helped dedicate a completed interstate segment in Big Horn County. *MDT.*

application would not be acceptable today. In 1971, the selection of Miss Montana Highways coincided with a legislative session at the state capitol building across the street from the highway department at Sixth Avenue and North Roberts Street. In an effort to attract legislators to an open house at the department, the state highway engineer suggested to Beverly Gibson of the department's Information Office that the building be kept open late because "we will have beautiful babes with mini-skirts!"

After interviewing the contenders on the morning of February 3, 1970, the judges selected nineteen-year-old Missoula native Sue Holloran as the first Miss Montana Highways. She was employed as a clerk-typist at the Missoula District office. During her reign, Holloran presided over several interstate openings, kicked off the annual summer litter campaign and also served as Miss Montana Highway 287. After she resigned in December 1970 to attend flight attendant school in Oregon, department administrators replaced Holloron with Kay Higgins, a Helena native and an employee of the old Gross Vehicle Weight Division. In July 1972, the judges selected Kitty Sullivan, a typist in the Accounting Bureau, for the distinction of

Miss Montana Highway. She was one of fourteen contestants that year for the honor of representing the highway department. The last woman to be so honored was Clarette "Buttons" LaSalle, a clerk-typist in the Helena headquarters building in Helena. A rising awareness of women's issues spelled the end of the Miss Montana Highways contest in late 1973.

While a footnote in the history of the MDT, Miss Montana Highways certainly represents a different era in the department's long history. In the early '70s, female employees served primarily in clerical roles and, except for the Advertising Department, didn't occupy managerial or professional positions. Miss Montana Highways was intended to put a prettier face on the highway department for functions where the media was often present. Today, women hold important managerial positions at the MDT as division administrators, bureau chiefs, section supervisors and engineers. To quote the old TV commercial, "You've come a long way, baby!"

# REFERENCES

*M*any of the chapters in this book came from articles originally written by the author for the Montana Department of Transportation's newsletter, *Newsline*. The articles were written from the early 2000s to 2019. They are included in this book with supplemental material and additional photographs. They are too numerous to list here and would detract from the use of the bibliography.

Axline, Jon. *Taming Big Sky Country: The History of Montana Transportation from Trails to Interstates*. Charleston, SC: The History Press, 2015.

Bird, Joan. *Montana UFOs and Extraterrestrials: Extraordinary Stories of Documented Sightings and Encounters*. Helena, MT: Riverbend Publishing, 2012.

Brown, Mark H. *Plainsmen of the Yellowstone: A History of the Yellowstone Basin*. New York: G.P. Putnam's Sons, 1961.

Burlingame, Merrill G. *The Montana Frontier*. Helena, MT: State Publishing Co., 1942.

Derleth, August. *The Milwaukee Road*. Iowa City: University of Iowa Press, 2002.

Federal Writers' Project. *Montana: A State Guide Book*. Helena: Montana Department of Agriculture, Labor and Industry, 1939.

Malone, Michael P., Richard B. Roeder and William L. Lang. *Montana: A History of Two Centuries*. Rev. ed. Seattle: University of Washington Press, 1991.

Montana State Highway Commission Meeting Minutes. Twenty-three vols. Director's office, Montana Department of Transportation, Helena, Montana.

Mullan, John. *Miners and Travelers Guide*. Fairfield, WA: Ye Galleon Press, n.d.

———. "Report on the Construction of a Military Road from Fort Walla Walla to Fort Benton." Reprint of 1863 Government Printing Office document. Fairfield, WA: Ye Galleon Press, 1994.

Niven, Francis. *Manhattan Omnibus*. Manhattan, MT: self-published, 1989.

Quivik, Fredric L. *Historic Bridges in Montana*. Washington, D.C.: Department of the Interior, 1982.

Vigilante Trail Association. *The Vigilante Trail*. Butte, MT: Murphy-Cheely, c. 1920.

Walter, David H., ed. *Speaking Ill of the Dead: Jerks in Montana History*. Second ed. Guilford, CT: Globe Pequot Press, 2011.

Zupan, Shirley, and Harry C. Owens. *Red Lodge: The Saga of a Western Area*. Red Lodge, MT: Carbon County Historical Society, 1979.

## *Historic American Building Survey (HABS)/Historic American Engineering Record (HAER) Documents*

Cyr Bridge. Mineral County. HAER No. MT-175.

Galetti Dairy. Silver Bow County. HABS No. MT-180.

Old Steel Bridge. Flathead County. HAER No. MT-21.

Rainbow Transmission Towers. Lewis and Clark County. HAER No. MT-172.

## *National Register of Historic Places Nominations (by author)*

Bearcreek Cemetery. NR# 11000017 (listed January 18, 2011).

Convict Grade Historic District. NR #15000485 (listed August 3, 2015).

Dude Rancher Lodge. NR #10000489 (listed July 22, 2010).

Jefferson Canyon Highway Historic District. NR #SG100002692 (listed July 23, 2018).

Lewis and Clark (Wolf Point) Bridge. NR #97001451 (listed November 24, 1997).

Milwaukee Road Railroad Substation No. 10 (Primrose). NR #14000394 (listed July 8, 2014).

Point of Rocks Historic Transportation Corridor–Mullan Road. NR #09000683 (listed September 4, 2009).

Pugsley Bridge (in progress, April 2020).

Smith Mine Historic District (with Joan Brownell). NR# 9000788 (listed September 30, 2009).

## *Newspapers*

*Anaconda Standard*
*Billings Gazette*
*Billings Herald*
*Bozeman Republican Courier*
*Butte Miner*
*Dillon Examiner*
*Great Falls Leader*
*Great Falls Tribune*
*Havre Daily News*
*Helena Independent*
*Helena Independent Record*
*Kalispell Daily Inter Lake*
*Kalispell Graphic*
*Manhattan Record*
*Missoulian*
*Montana Citizen* (Glasgow)
*Montana Standard* (Butte)
*Red Lodge Picket*
*Searchlight* (Culbertson)
*Wolf Point Herald*

# INDEX

# ABOUT THE AUTHOR

*J*on Axline is the longtime historian at the Montana Department of Transportation. When not sweating over the state's historic roads and bridges, he conducts cultural resource surveys and writes the MDT's roadside historical and geological interpretive markers. Jon was a regular contributor to *Montana Magazine* and *Montana: The Magazine of Western History*. He is the author of *Conveniences Sorely Needed: Montana's Historic Highway Bridges*, as well as the editor of *Montana's Historical Highway Markers*, *Taming Big Sky Country: A History of Montana Transportation from Trails to Interstates* and *The Beartooth Highway: A History of America's Most Beautiful Drive*. With Ellen Baumler, he wrote *Hidden History of Helena, Montana* in 2019. Jon lives in Helena with his wife and four dogs.